RESEARCHING YOUR IRISH ANCESTORS AT HOME AND ABROAD

DAVID R. ELLIOTT

DUNDURN
TORONTO

Editor: Ruth Chernia
Copy Editor: Matt Baker
Design: Jennifer Scott
Printer: Marquis

Library and Archives Canada Cataloguing in Publication

Elliott, David Raymond, 1948-
    Researching your Irish ancestors at home and abroad / David R. Elliott.

Includes bibliographical references and index.
Issued also in electronic formats.
ISBN 978-1-4597-0397-1

    1. Ireland--Genealogy--Handbooks, manuals, etc. I. Title.

CS483.E45 2012   929.1072'0415   C2011-908036-2

1   2   3   4   5   16   15   14   13   12

We acknowledge the support of the Canada Council for the Arts and the Ontario Arts Council for our publishing program. We also acknowledge the financial support of the Government of Canada through the Canada Book Fund and Livres Canada Books, and the Government of Ontario through the Ontario Book Publishing Tax Credit and the Ontario Media Development Corporation.

Care has been taken to trace the ownership of copyright material used in this book. The author and the publisher welcome any information enabling them to rectify any references or credits in subsequent editions.

                                                                                            J. Kirk Howard, President

Printed and bound in Canada.
www.dundurn.com

Ontario Genealogical Society
Suite 102, 40 Orchard View Boulevard
Toronto, Ontario, Canada M4R 1B9
tel. (416) 489-0734   fax. (416) 489-9803
provoffice@ogs.on.ca   www.ogs.on.ca

Dundurn	Gazelle Book Services Limited	Dundurn
3 Church Street, Suite 500	White Cross Mills	2250 Military Road
Toronto, Ontario, Canada	High Town, Lancaster, England	Tonawanda, NY
M5E 1M2	LA1 4XS	U.S.A. 14150

RESEARCHING YOUR IRISH ANCESTORS AT HOME AND ABROAD

CONTENTS

ACKNOWLEDGEMENTS

In doing my research in Ireland, I have learned greatly from the important tips and prior research of friends and genealogy speakers: Sunday Thompson, Richard Doherty, Elayne Lockhart, and John Grenham. I also owe much to Valerie Adams — formerly of PRONI and now librarian of the Presbyterian Historical Society in Belfast — for her friendship and the support of our work.

Many thanks go to the staff members at PRONI, whom I came to know while delivering genealogical training lectures there. Having a personal relationship with archival staff always makes the research go much easier. The National Archives and National Library in Dublin also went out of their way to give assistance. Formerly with the Enniskillen Public Library and now with the library system in County Tyrone, Margaret Kane was an important resource in my early research in County Fermanagh.

I have been privileged to lecture to the County Fermanagh Family History Society and have learned much from its members; I cherish their friendship, especially Viola Wiggins, Frank McHugh, Mervyn Hall, and P.J. O'Brien, who have been my resources "on the ground," answering questions and even taking photographs for me when I needed them immediately for a report. Not to be forgotten is Vynette Sage, a society member in Arizona who has done so much in making County Fermanagh records available online.

Over the past eight years, my research for clients has taken me to places in Ireland that I might not have visited otherwise. I thank these individuals for giving me the opportunity to experience so much of Ireland and discover rare documents in its various archives.

My wife and I have been hosted by Val and David Bailey at Blaney Caravan Park and Camp Site. David has shared his vast local knowledge of the area and has put us in contract with many helpful people. We are indebted to Laura and Derek Elliott for their friendship and assistance in many of our genealogical projects. Peter O'Shaughnessy of Roundwood Caravan Park and Campground in County Wicklow has been our host on several occasions and has also put us in touch with knowledgeable people in his area.

A special thanks to the various archives and agencies that have allowed us to reproduce documents to illustrate this book. Also, Susan Smart of the York branch of the Ontario Genealogical Society kindly provided an Orange Lodge transfer certificate as an illustration.

I wish to acknowledge Fraser Dunford, past executive director of the Ontario Genealogical Society, and my publisher Kirk Howard at Dundurn Press for encouraging me to write this book. Ruth Chernia, editor with the OGS, and Matt Baker from Dundurn guided the manuscript to its publication.

This book is dedicated to my wife, Nancy, who initially encouraged me to explore my ancestry, has worked in Irish cemeteries and archives with me, and prepared the maps for this book.

INTRODUCTION

Sometimes, people from North America or Australia, the major areas for Irish emigration, walk into the National Library or National Archives in Dublin — or the Public Records Office of Northern Ireland in Belfast (PRONI) — looking for their Irish ancestors, expecting to have their genealogy handed to them on a plate. Such expectation is just as unrealistic as it would be in similar institutions in their home country. They perceive the archivists to be omniscient! It must be remembered that many of the front-line archival staff are civil servants without formal training in history or genealogy — some have no interest in either. Fortunately, since the availability of the Irish 1901 and 1911 censuses, more civil servants have been catching the genealogy bug and are becoming more knowledgeable. You may have more knowledge of genealogy than they do; however, they know how their archives work and can be a great resource if you know what you are looking for.

Unless you know the county and parish of your ancestors before you go to an Irish archival institution, you will be disappointed. The key to successful genealogical work in Ireland is homework *prior* to going to Ireland. This book is designed to help you identify the county and parish of your ancestors using documents and Internet sites in your home country. Your ancestors left paper trails, and it is important to examine all of those leads in order to identify, or at least narrow down, the Irish counties they came from, thus allowing you to begin your search in the various Irish archives.

Some people give up on Irish genealogical research because they have been told that so many of the important documents were destroyed. It is true that certain Irish documents were destroyed in the 1922 Four Courts fire, but many others have survived and they may have information on your ancestors. Irish genealogical research is probably one of the most difficult areas, but if done properly and consistently, it can be very rewarding.

This book is not exhaustive but will help steer you in right direction on how to do your research at home and in Ireland. To begin, it outlines the political and religious history of Ireland, which has had a great bearing on genealogical research and the type of surviving documents. It will then, as mentioned, explain how to use non-Irish sources to discover your ancestor's county of origin. This will reduce your search from thirty-two counties down to one for each of your ancestral lines. After that, you should be collecting as much information as you can about the parish they lived in so that you can plan your research trip ahead of time. There are practical tips on travel in Ireland, various budget accommodations, and plenty of advice on how to get the most out of your research trip.

The major archival institutions in Ireland are introduced with the resources they hold, and there is also a chapter on researching Irish cemeteries. A genealogical checklist will help you organize your research, and an annotated bibliography of the best printed and electronic sources has been provided.

Many of the research facilities that you may wish to visit do not cross the radar of local residents. I have found that locals and even cops on the beat did not know the locations of archives that were only a few feet from them in Belfast and Londonderry. To help you find your way, I have included maps and photographs of the important archival buildings.

Over the past year (2011–12), three important genealogical repositories in Belfast have changed their addresses, as has the National Map Centre in Dublin — information on the addresses of the new facilities and how they work has been included. I have also provided listings for their websites that you should check for hours of operation and other matters. The web addresses were accurate as of the end of February 2012.

This book is intended as a treasure map that you should take with you to Ireland on your genealogical quest. For those who have non-genealogical spouses, there is much to occupy them in the many museums, art galleries, theatres, historic prisons, castles, heritage sites, and shopping centres in Dublin and Belfast while you are doing your ancestry thing. They even may catch your enthusiasm for things Irish!

CHAPTER ONE

Understanding Religion and Politics in Ireland

Religion and politics have a complicated history in Ireland, and this has had a major impact on the generation and condition of its genealogical records. Understanding the relationship between Irish politics and the churches will help you in your search.

Although the Romans knew of Ireland and Ptolemy mapped some of its southern coast, they never occupied it. Christianity came to Ireland largely through the efforts of Catholic missionaries in the fourth century. Gradually, the monastic orders were able to establish Catholic churches throughout the island, although vestiges of the earlier Druid religion persisted.

As the Roman Empire disintegrated in Europe, Ireland became an outpost of Western civilization; the Christian monks were busy copying religious and classical texts. This is well-documented in Thomas Cahill's *How the Irish Saved Civilization* and Sir Kenneth Clark's *Civilization* series. Celtic monks eventually went as missionaries to continental Europe to evangelize and educate the Franks, Jutes, Vikings, and other "barbarians" who had taken over northern Europe.

As Vikings advanced their attacks on Ireland in the ninth century, the monks were forced to move their monasteries to

Skellig Michael, County Kerry. This was a monastic settlement from the sixth to twelfth centuries on this isolated island off the west coast of Ireland. Here Christian monks copied scripture and classical works, helping to save western civilization.

rocky islands to the west, but even those outposts were seized by the Vikings. Eventually, some of the Vikings were converted to Christianity, and by the tenth century, they began settling in Ireland, establishing towns such as Shannon, Limerick, Cork, and Dublin.

NORMANS

The next invasion of Ireland occurred when the Norman King John of England occupied it in the twelfth century and divided its land among his relatives and retainers. This period saw several large changes in Ireland:

- Many castles were created to consolidate Norman power and resist further Viking attacks.
- Large cathedrals based on gothic architectural models were established throughout the island.
- The Norman system of parishes was introduced, and residents were required to pay tithes (10 percent of their produce, often in kind) to support the Catholic Church.

TUDORS

When Henry VIII broke with the pope and set himself up as the head of the Church of England in 1534, this eventually made him the head of the Church of Ireland in 1536. Henry seized the monasteries of Ireland, taking their treasures for him self, and sold off most of the monastic properties. Many of the medieval church records were destroyed as monastic libraries were pillaged.

Under Henry, the Church of Ireland became an arm of the British establishment. Its offices were filled by persons loyal to Henry. The form of worship changed little, except for the fact that Henry made the decisions rather than the pope. Marriages were regulated by the state.

During the reign of Henry's son Edward VI, the Church of England and the Church of Ireland took on a more Protestant character. The Protestant transformation of the Church of Ireland was completed during the reign of Henry's daughter Elizabeth I. It became the state, or established, church; its services were governed by the Anglican *Book of Common Prayer*, and all citizens of Ireland were expected to attend its services.

Elizabeth settled groups of English and Scottish Protestant "planters" in the north and south in order to establish a Protestant culture in Ireland, and penal laws were enacted against Catholics. Many were driven from their lands, and they were excluded from education and official positions. As a result, Catholic services went underground, mass being clandestinely celebrated out in the forests and glens; large rocks were used as altars. Under such hardships, few Catholic records were generated. Some Catholics, however, converted to the Church of Ireland in order to keep their lands and their positions.

The process of importing Protestant loyalists continued under James I. Vast amounts of Catholic-owned lands were seized and given to British military officers and politicians, who became a new class of absentee landlords. During this period, the Protestant "ascendancy" built many more castles in order to protect their interests. Church of Ireland members were in the numerical minority, but they now held most of the land and political power. Not only did the church control baptisms, marriages, and burials, but the Church of Ireland courts also probated wills and administered social welfare. It even operated most of the graveyards; everyone, including Catholics, could be buried in them, but there might be a special section for Catholics.

1641 REBELLION AND CROMWELL

In 1641 Irish Catholics revolted against the British overlords and civil war broke out in Ireland. Widespread killing of Protestants transpired, particularly in Ulster. This happened during the period that the pro-Catholic King Charles I was battling parliament. After Charles was beheaded, Oliver Cromwell, the megalomaniac dictator who now ruled England, sought to make an example of Ireland, claiming that he was guided by God. His troops invaded Ireland in 1649, burning some Catholics alive in their churches and driving the remainder to the western counties of Ireland. Cromwell gave them little choice: "To hell or Connemara," which was a rocky region on the west coast of Ireland.

Tully Castle, County Fermanagh, destroyed during the 1641 uprising. One of the many castles built by British planters at the beginning of the seventeenth century.

It has been estimated that between 25 and 50 percent of Ireland's population died in the conflict or from the associated disruption of agriculture and resulting famine. In addition, many Irish were sent as slaves to Barbados. Again, vast amounts of the land of Ireland were given to Cromwell's soldiers in lieu of salaries.

WILLIAM OF ORANGE

About forty years later, Ireland was again beset by British political struggles. King James II, who was pro-Catholic, was supported by Irish Catholics. English Protestants sided with his son-in-law, William of Orange. Their armies clashed throughout Ireland, but Protestant forces of William of Orange were triumphant in

Castle Coole, Enniskillen, County Fermanagh. One of the Palladian mansions of the super-rich landlords.

the decisive Battle of the Boyne, which was fought in County Meath in 1690.

Under William's rule of Ireland, heavier penal laws were imposed on Catholics. In addition to denying Catholics voting privileges, these laws prevented them from entering the professions, getting educations, possessing arms, using the Gaelic language, and forbade Roman Catholic church services. Further complicating matters, the Church of Ireland probate courts interfered with Catholic wills, applying primogeniture if the eldest son converted to Anglicanism or dividing the estate among all siblings if he did not. Eventually, Roman Catholic land ownership dropped to 5 percent of the land mass of Ireland — the rest was owned primarily by absentee British landlords. William's reign saw the creation of vast estates and palatial mansions such as Powerscourt, Castletown, Strokestown Estate, Florence Court, and Castle Coole, often rivalling European palaces.

The Church of Ireland remained the state church in Ireland, and its clergy were often the sons of British aristocrats, many of whom had a sense of entitlement. Its rectors were commonly the resident magistrates, who adjudicated the local courts. Attendance at Trinity College Dublin, founded in 1592, the only university in Ireland at the time, was limited to members of the Church of Ireland (Anglicans). Civil service positions were likewise closed to all but Anglicans; even Presbyterians were barred from public office.

Other types of Protestants, including Baptists and Quakers, who had come to Ireland as "planters" under Elizabeth and James, also found themselves as second-class citizens. Dissenters or nonconformists often had to practise their religion in secret. Baptists and Quakers, who did not practise infant baptism, avoided one of the problems of the state church, but they still had to seek the services of the Church of Ireland for marriages.

Church of Ireland marriage record, 1838, Fivemiletown, Clogher Parish, County Tyrone.

BAPTISMS.

(The Year 1807)   Page 7

Courtesy of PRONI and the Deputy Keeper of the Records.

1801

Burried

Jan. 30. Catherine Taylor alias Balfour aged 27

Feb. 20. Mary Davis aged 18

Mar. 7. Mary Cox aged 45

— 13. George Strong aged 80

Ap. 15. Mary Brown aged 48

16. Jane Maguire aged 40

19. James Fallis aged 65

20. Mary Brownlee aged 70

— Grace Saunderson aged 37

30. Catherine Irwin aged 61

May 3. James Tarrel aged 43

June 29. John Henderson aged 76

Left: *Church of Ireland baptismal register, 1807–08, Fivemiletown, Clogher Parish, County Tyrone.*

Above: *Church of Ireland burial register, 1801, Devenish Parish, County Fermanagh. Some registers give few details.*

PRESBYTERIANS

Presbyterians, whose religion was the established church in Scotland, faced severe restrictions on their religious and civil life in Ireland. They might hold religious services, but they could not call their buildings churches; they were called meeting houses instead, as were the sanctuaries of other dissenters. Presbyterian ministers were not allowed to perform marriages until 1782, and they could not perform mixed marriages between Presbyterians and persons of other denominations until 1845, when civil registration of marriages began. As a result, baptisms, marriages, and burials of Presbyterians can often be found in the local Church of Ireland parish registers.

Presbyterian baptismal register, 1836–38, Clogher Presbyterian Church, County Tyrone. Note that the mothers were not listed.

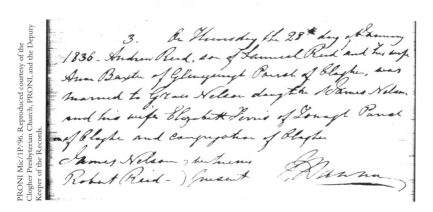

Presbyterian marriage record, 1836, Clogher Presbyterian Church, County Tyrone. This record included more genealogical information than the later civil registrations.

In 1798, inspired by the American and French revolutions, some Presbyterians joined the Catholics in trying to throw off the yoke of Britain and the Church of Ireland to set up a democratic republic. With much bloodshed, this rebellion was severely crushed, and some rebel Presbyterian ministers from Ulster were hanged from the roofs of their meeting houses.

METHODISM

Methodism was founded by John and Charles Wesley, both Church of England ministers. On repeated trips to Ireland in the second half of the eighteenth century, John Wesley established Methodist societies that were devoted to Bible study, evangelism among the poor, and religious reform. He intended for Methodist societies to be an arm of the Church of Ireland.

After John Wesley's death in 1791, Methodists in England and Ireland experienced a number of internal schisms over their relationship to the state church. Ironically, those calling themselves Wesleyan Methodists (Wesley was an Anglican until his death) decided in

1816 to set up their own churches and perform their own baptisms separate from the Church of Ireland. Primitive Methodists, however, remained loyal to the Church of Ireland. Most Wesleyan Methodist baptismal registers start in the 1830s, and marriages were only performed after 1845, when civil registration began.

Methodist ministers often travelled a large circuit and performed baptisms while on their rounds, even for the children of non-Methodists if the Church of Ireland minister was not

Methodist baptismal register, 1843–44, Ballyshannon Circuit, Counties Donegal and Fermanagh.

available. If you are looking for Methodist baptismal entries for a specific place, you are likely to find them among the Methodist circuit records or in the local Church of Ireland baptismal records.

QUAKERS

The Quakers, or Religious Society of Friends, kept detailed records of births, marriages, and deaths for members of their religious community and some of their neighbours. Most of their registers dating back to the mid-seventeenth century have survived.

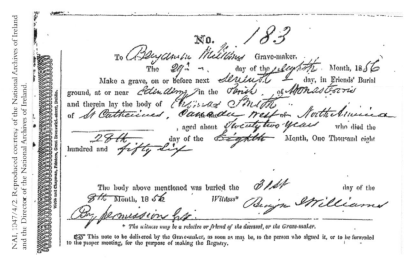

Quaker burial order, 1856, Queen's County. This was for a Canadian from St. Catharines, Canada West, who had died while in Ireland.

CATHOLICS

The lifting of the penal laws against Catholics in the late 1820s finally allowed Roman Catholics to practise their faith openly. Although there are Catholic Church registers that exist from the late 1600s, most Catholic parish registers start after the penal laws were removed.

PROBLEMS WITH IRISH PARISH REGISTERS

The parish registers of the various denominations varied from time to time and were not always filled out completely, even when columns were provided for particular information. Prior to civil registration, the baptismal registers of the Church of Ireland and Catholic Church often gave the names of the parents, but not always the maiden names of the mothers. You will find some registers list only the name of the father of the child being baptized. In many cases, the townland was indicated. In the case of marriage registers, the names of the parents are not normally given. Burial records usually give date of burial, age, and townland.

Due to the incomplete data in the parish registers, genealogical linking becomes difficult. In the absence of census records, the townland becomes a very important tool in identifying people, but even then, because several families of the same surname often lived on the same townland and cousins often shared forenames, you need to be very careful in linking marriage records to birth records.

TITHE APPLOTMENTS

One aspect of the established church regulations that has a bearing upon genealogical research was the process of collecting tithes, a religious tax to support the Church of Ireland. In 1823 there was a shift from collecting tithes in kind to collecting monetary tithes. Church of Ireland ministers were required to assess all of the townlands in their parishes to determine their size and yield, then affix an appropriate amount of tithe upon each of the tenants.

The tithe applotment books usually list each townland and the names of each of the heads of the households. They become a partial census substitute. However, those who were living in towns, cities, or on church lands were not assessed. Nor are cottiers, who sublet small cottages from lease holders and often worked as labourers, likely to show up in the tithe records. In some cases, large land-owners collected the tithes themselves and hired the ministers, so the householder names did not appear in the church tithe records, otherwise the Church of Ireland ministers had to collect the tithes from the people. The tithe applotment books have been micro-filmed and there is a partial index of them now on *www.ancestry.com*.

Many non-Anglicans regarded the tithes as an unwanted religious tax: they may have already been supporting their own

A portion of a tithe applotment page, 1824, Ballybeg Townland, Ferns Parish, County Wexford. Land was assessed for size and quality and the tithe was demanded by the Church of Ireland.

dissenter church, whether Protestant or Catholic. In the 1830s, there were revolts against the collection of tithes. Eneclann has published a collection of records on CD-ROM pertaining to tithe defaulters in the southern counties of Ireland, giving the names, addresses, and occupations of many of those who refused to pay the tithes. Included are some interesting affidavits by the tithe collectors and witnesses that provide important socio-historical context. In 1838 the tithe collection was removed from tenants and placed on landlords, who increased the cost of rent in order to cover the cost of the tithes they had to pay to the church.

ORDNANCE SURVEY

In the 1830s, the British government began a complete mapping of Ireland for military and taxation purposes, showing the natural features and the buildings on each townland. The resulting Ordnance Survey maps are important for genealogists and historians as they study the past. Army engineers also prepared extensive reports on each parish, detailing the geological and botanic features of the properties, information on health and social customs, churches, schools, emigrants, important officials, and they drew pictures of noteworthy buildings. Some farmers, schoolteachers, and other people were also identified in certain localities. Forty volumes of the *Ordnance Survey Memoirs* have been prepared by scholars at Queen's University, Belfast, and have been published by the Ulster Historical Foundation. There is also a large index volume available that lists the names of those mentioned.

NATIONAL SCHOOLS

After 1831, national schools came into existence and standardized education across Ireland. Although the national schools were intended to be non-sectarian, Catholic clergy, who had previously filled an educational role in some schools, continued to do so under the new system, with their salaries provided by state funding. Registers from after 1860 survive, and they contain the names and ages of the pupils as well as the names and occupations of their fathers. Often those registers indicate what happened to the pupils after they left the school.

POOR LAW UNIONS

In 1838 the British government established poor law unions throughout Ireland to administer social welfare. Several poor law unions could exist in a county, and they often extended over county lines. For example, the Enniskillen Poor Law Union served parts of Fermanagh, Cavan, and Tyrone.

Each of the poor law unions maintained a workhouse and a fever hospital for the poor, and entering the workhouses was the only way they could receive any assistance. Each of these unions was administered by a board of guardians, which was made up of local gentry, clergy, and medical personnel. The minute books of the Guardians and the registers that the poor law unions generated are important sources of social history and genealogy.

PARISH RELIGIOUS CENSUSES

From time to time, the Church of Ireland undertook enumerations of people in their parishes. The Diocese of Elphin did a listing of people in 1659, and the Diocese of Meath did a similar census in 1802–03.

In 1841 the rector for Devenish Parish of the Church of Ireland in County Fermanagh used a printed form to record the enumeration of those within the parish. The census included the names of family members, their relationships, occupations, and townlands, but no ages. Primarily Protestants were listed, but occasionally a Catholic family was included.

In 1851 the rector updated his copy of the 1841 census by annotating it, recording who was still there as well as new residents. He also noted those who had married, died, or moved away, including the associated dates and sometimes where they had moved to. This document was then updated again in 1861.

While not all of the surviving parish censuses are as detailed as the one for Devenish parish, and not all of them have survived, it is wise to consult local churches and major archives to see if they possess them.

A page from the Devenish Parish annotated religious census, 1841–1861.

GREAT FAMINE 1845–1852

Ireland was again struck by misfortune in 1845 — the Great Famine. To understand its impact, one needs to understand the system of land tenure. Most of the Irish did not own their own land; they were tenant farmers who rented from the landowners. They paid their rents in kind, and up to two-thirds of their increase went to the landlord. Much of the harvest was sold abroad. To supplement their own food supply, the poor planted potatoes in any spare ground they could find. Potatoes became the staple of their diet.

In 1845 an imported fungus destroyed most of the potato plants, and the result was widespread starvation. The British government refused to modify the export laws so that foodstuffs could be retained in Ireland or imported, because it did not want to disrupt the international economic markets. This attitude further alienated the Irish from their British overlords, who were seen as practising genocide.

When tenants could not pay their rent because they were hungry, sick, and could not work, they were expelled from their properties. Sometimes their cottages were torched by landlords so they could not come back. For those desperate enough, the only way to get assistance was to enter the dreaded workhouses, which became a virtual death sentence because of widespread disease inside these institutions. By late 1847, there were over one million inmates in the crowded workhouses. Late that year, it was decided to extend relief to the poor who were living in their own homes. This was called outdoor relief and it began in 1848. Consequently, poor law unions kept outdoor relief ledgers, and while not all of these records have survived, those that do are full of genealogical information and townlands are given in most cases.

By the end of the famine in 1852, about 1.5 million Irish had died from the famine and spread of disease. At one workhouse in

An Enniskillen Poor Law Union outdoor relief register, 1848.

Skibbereen, County Cork, there were over ten thousand buried in a mass grave, a practice that became common. Often, the only memorial to those who died in the workhouses is to be found in the surviving workhouse registers.

Over 1.5 million Irish immigrated to Britain, North America, and the Antipodes (Australia and New Zealand) during the famine in order to find a better existence. Some landlords paid their tenants' travel expenses so as to remove them from their responsibility. Many died aboard the disease-infested "coffin" ships, where cholera, typhus, and dysentery were rampant.

CIVIL REGISTRATION

The year 1845 also saw the beginning of civil registration of marriages in Ireland. While this option was initially extended to Protestants, Catholics were afforded the same opportunity in 1864, when civil registrations for all births and deaths similarly began. This made marriage services outside of church possible; they could now be performed in the local registry offices without the benefit of clergy.

Examples of birth, marriage, and death civil registrations.

Available at the General Register Office, yearly indexes covering all of Ireland allow for easy searching of births, deaths, and marriages. They were a great improvement over the parish registers, which are often inconsistent. Note that christening and burial records do not usually provide birth or death dates. It is also important to remember that not all vital events were recorded, either because of non-compliance or the loss of documents between the local register offices and the General Register Office. Sometimes, the missing events can be found in the parish registers — if they survived.

Civil birth registrations give the name of the baby, the parents (including the maiden name of the mother), the occupation of the father, and the townland. Marriage registrations give the townlands of the parties and the names and occupations of spouses, as well as their fathers' names and occupations. Death registrations give the date, townland, occupation, cause of death, and the name (and often relationship) of the informant.

GRIFFITH'S PRIMARY VALUATION (1848–64)

In 1848 a systematic survey of Ireland was undertaken. *Griffith's Primary Valuation of Land* enumerated each head of household on each townland, listed the landowner or middleman, the size of the properties, and linked the residents to the numbered portions of the earlier Ordnance Survey maps. The survey began at Dublin in 1848 and travelled in a general clockwise fashion around the island. As the counties were surveyed, the results were printed in bound volumes. The names of the persons and the townlands in the *Griffith's Valuation* have been thoroughly indexed and the images digitized. They can be found on several websites, including *www.askaboutireland.ie* and *www.irishorigins. com*. The latter site has a better search engine, but you have to buy a subscription.

Because Griffith's was an evaluation of agricultural land, you are not likely to find the names of those living in towns and villages, or tradesmen or farm employees who might have sublet part of a rural property. Yet, this is an important census substitute.

138   **VALUATION OF TENEMENTS.**

PARISH OF ROSSORRY.

No. and Letters of Reference to Map.	Names.		Description of Tenement.	Area.	Rateable Annual Valuation.		Total Annual Valuation of Rateable Property.
	Townlands and Occupiers.	Immediate Lessors.			Land.	Buildings.	
	LENAGHAN. (Ord. S. 21.)			A. R. P.	£ s. d.	£ s. d.	£ s. d.
1	Maurice C. Maude,	Marquis of Ely,	House, offices, and land,	56 0 30	45 0 0	60 0 0	105 0 0
2	Marquis of Ely,	In fee,	Land,	5 3 22	3 15 0	—	3 15 0
3	Richard Gamble.	Marquis of Ely,	Herd's ho., off., & land,	70 1 0	46 15 0	1 0 0	47 15 0
4	Thomas Guthridge,	Same,	Herd's ho., off., & land,	33 1 10	22 10 0	0 10 0	23 0 0
5			Water,	2 2 8	—		
			Total,	166 0 30	118 0 0	61 10 0	179 10 0
	LURGANDARRAGH, LITTLE. (Ord. S. 21.)						
1	John Wordsworth,	Marquis of Ely,	House, offices, and land,	38 2 2	29 10 0	2 0 0	31 10 0
2	Thomas Wordsworth,	Same,	House and land,	2 1 30	2 5 0	0 15 0	3 0 0
			Total,	40 3 32	31 15 0	2 15 0	34 10 0
	MOYGLASS. (Ord. S. 21.)						
1	Aaron Dundas,	Marquis of Ely,	House, offices, and land,	52 1 0	49 0 0	3 10 0	52 10 0
2	Robert Dundas,	Same,	House, offices, and land,	16 1 18	15 15 0	2 5 0	18 0 0
			Total,	68 2 18	64 15 0	5 15 0	70 10 0
	PORTNUSH. (Ord. S. 21.)						
1	John Mitchell,	Marquis of Ely,	Herd's house and land,	44 0 0	26 10 0	0 5 0	26 15 0
2	James Palmer,	Same,	House, offices, and land,	14 3 25	9 15 0	1 5 0	11 0 6
3	George Elliott,	Same,	House, office, and land,	13 2 3	9 15 0	1 0 0	10 15 0
4	William Elliott,	Same,	Land,	40 1 0	28 0 0	—	28 0 0
			Total,	112 1 28	74 0 0	2 10 0	76 10 0
	RATONA. (Ord. S. 21.)						
1	Marquis of Ely,	In fee,	Herd's ho., offs., & land,	59 3 0	44 10 0	1 10 0	46 0 0
2	Baptist Gamble,	Marquis of Ely,	Herd's house and land,	40 0 10	55 0 0	1 0 0	56 0 0
3 a	Maurice C. Maude,	Same,	Gate-house and land,	50 2 5	47 10 0	2 0 0	49 10 0
— b	Unoccupied,	Maurice C. Maude,	Clerk's house,	1 2 3	—	5 0 0	5 0 0
4	Michael Boland,	Marquis of Ely,	House, office, and land,	20 0 7	15 0 0	1 0 0	16 0 0
5 A	William Bothwell,	Same,	House, offices, & land,	15 3 36	12 0 0	1 0 0	19 0 0
— B				6 2 35	6 0 0		
6			Water,	1 1 23	—	—	—
			Total,	198 0 20	180 0 0	11 10 0	191 10 0
	RIGG, (Ord. S. 21.)						
1	Thomas Arthur,	Marquis of Ely,	House, offices, and land,	16 0 5	10 15 0	0 15 0	11 10 0
2	James Arthur,	Same,	House, offices, and land,	37 2 20	31 0 0	1 10 0	32 10 0
3 A	Andrew Arthur,	Same,	House, offices, & land,	16 2 5	9 0 0	0 15 0	11 0 0
— B				1 2 3	1 5 0		
4 A	James Blake,	Same,	House, offices, & land,	20 1 25	22 0 0	1 10 0	25 0 0
— B				1 3 15	1 10 0		
5	Thomas Guthridge,	Same,	House, offices, and land,	37 3 20	29 10 0	3 10 0	33 0 0
6	Edward Lunney,	Same,	House, offices, and land,	20 3 25	20 10 0	1 10 0	22 0 0
7 a	Hugh Roberts,	Same,	House, offices, and land,	62 0 30	45 0 0	1 0 0	46 0 0
— b	Mary Amos,	Hugh Roberts,	House,	—	—	0 10 0	0 10 0
			Total,	232 3 28	163 10 0	11 0 0	174 10 0
	DRUMGALLAN. (Ord. S. 27 & 22.)						
1 A	John Hoye,	James Clarke,	Land,	3 2 30	3 10 0	—	8 10 0
— B				5 3 5	5 0 0		
2	Daniel Donnelly,	Same,	Land,	9 1 15	10 0 0	—	10 0 0
3	Thomas Smyth,	Same,	House, office, & land,	7 2 30	7 15 0	0 15 0	16 10 0
4	John Carleton,	Same,	House, office, and land,	10 1 5	8 0 0		6 0 0
5	John Smyth,	Same,	Land,	5 3 5	4 10 0	1 10 0	6 0 0
6	Edward Murphy,	Same,	House, offices, and land,	1 0 5	1 0 0	—	1 0 0
7				19 2 30	16 15 0	2 5 0	19 0 0

An example of the Griffith's Valuation, *circa 1860, Rossorry Parish, County Fermanagh. Land was assessed for size and quality and rated for taxation.*

In the years following the *Griffith's Valuation*, yearly updates were made in the land books as tenants changed, new leases were issued, or land was sold. These entries were recorded with various coloured inks. These cancellation books or revision books, as they are variously called, are found in the Valuation Office in Dublin and PRONI in Belfast.

DISESTABLISHMENT OF THE CHURCH OF IRELAND, 1871

At the end of 1870, the Church of Ireland ceased to be the state church. This was the result of growing liberal attitudes in Britain that saw state churches as an anachronism. Because the Church of Ireland records had been created by a state institution, its records to the end of 1870 were ordered to be deposited in the Public Records Office in Dublin. These included the christening, marriage, and burial records, as well as marriage bonds and probated wills prior to 1858. It was intended that the Public Records Office would ensure their survival. This proved to be wishful thinking.

As the Church of Ireland was disestablished, some nine hundred church glebe lands were sold off to the tenants. These had previously provided revenue to the clergy and involved about eleven thousand tenants. Mortgages were provided by the state, and these sales created a new class of landowners in Ireland.

CENSUS RECORDS

Nominal censuses, which listed everyone in the household, had been taken in Ireland from 1821 onward in ten-year intervals. Around 1878 the British government ordered that the 1861 and 1871 census returns be destroyed so that they could not be used "for the satisfaction of curiosity," perhaps out of sensitivity to the way Irish affairs had been handled during and after the Famine.

No. 77 Townland of *Irvinestown* in the Parish of *Derryvollan*

N. B. In Counties where Plowlands or other denominations or sub-denominations are in use, the word " Townlands"

Col. 1. No. of House.	Col. 2. No. of Stories	Column 3. NAMES OF INHABITANTS.	Col. 4. AGE.	Column 5. OCCUPATION.
		John *Kelly his Son*	4	
24	1	George Ramsay	25	Labourer
		Martha D°. Wife	22	
		Mary D°. daughter	1	
25	1	James Leonard	55	Taylor
		Jane D°. Wife	50	
		James D°. Son	19	
		Henry D°. D°.	17	
		Andrew D°. D°.	14	
		Mary D°. Daughter	11	
		Jane D°. D°.	7	
26	1	James Allen	40	Weaver
		John D°. Son	19	
		Andrew D°. D°.	17	
		James D°. D°.	15	
		William d°. d°.	6	
27	1	Mary Kennedy	59	Widow and Flax Spinner
		Ann Dixon Daughter	33	
		Eliza Binny daughter	29	
		Abraham Dixon Grandson	15	
		Mary Jane Grand Daughter	11	
		Eliza d° d°	7	
28	1	William Elliott	24	Reedmaker
		Rebecca d°. Wife	25	
		Alexander D°. Son	2	

An example of the 1821 census, Derryvullan Parish, County Fermanagh.

Also, there was a paper drive during the First World War, and through a misunderstanding, the government in Dublin pulped the 1881 and 1891 census returns.

Fortunately, the 1901 and 1911 census records were preserved and eventually digitized with the help of the Archives of Canada. You can find them online from the National Archives of Ireland. The 1861 census differed from the British census in that it listed the religion of those enumerated. It appears that the Canadian model was used, having a divided culture: English/French and Protestant/Catholic. By listing religion, the British authorities were able to estimate the potential resistance, as Irish nationalism was on the rise. The listing of religion continued in the subsequent Irish censuses.

The 1901 and 1911 censuses continued the practice of also including the name of the birth county of those enumerated. This is of help in trying to trace family origins.

THE FOUR COURTS FIRE, 1922

Resistance to Britain's rule came to a head in 1916 with the Easter Uprising, when Irish Republican Army (IRA) tried to drive out the British. After heavy fighting, Britain agreed to home rule for Ireland in 1921, and an Irish government, in conjunction with Westminster, was formed with Michael Collins as its head. Six counties in Ulster would not accept this and remained under delegated British rule as Northern Ireland.

Militant members of the IRA refused to accept the new Irish rule, seeing it as an unworthy compromise, and declared war on Collins's government. The rebels seized control of the Public Records Office at the Four Courts and made it their headquarters, establishing a munitions dump inside the records vault. When the Irish government forces fired upon the building, the munitions blew up and burned almost all of the records, including over a thousand Church of Ireland parish registers, the marriage bonds, the probated pre-1858 wills, and the remaining 1821 to 1851 census returns.

This was to be the final insult to Irish historical records. Fortunately, over six hundred Church of Ireland parish registers had not been sent in to the Public Records Office, because they were still being used or copies had been made. Only four parish registers were salvaged from the fire at the Public Records Office.

Indexes of the marriage bonds and pre-1858 wills had also been made and were held off-site. Similarly, an index of the heads of households in Dublin had been done and was held off-site. Some census fragments were salvaged and copies of the some of the pre-1901 census returns have been found in local churches. Archives in Dublin and Belfast have copies of these census fragments, and Eneclann and the Ottawa Branch of the Ontario Genealogical Society have published parts of the 1851 census.

IRISH PENSION APPLICATIONS

Some of the 1841 and 1851 census information has survived because copies had been kept off-site from the Four Courts. An example of this comes from the old-age pension program, which Irish government adopted in 1908. For those who could not provide documentation of their birth date, the surviving census records for 1841 and 1851 were consulted by pension officials. Abstracts of some of the 1841 and 1851 census returns had been held in the pension office, and copies of those documents can be found at PRONI and the National Archives of Ireland. Some have been put online, and for a fee, you can obtain copies of what you find at *www.ireland-genealogy.com*.

Just as the earlier census records were searched to establish proof of age, so, too, were Church of Ireland parish registers. The results of those searches are in the National Archives.

An example of an Old Age Pension search of the 1851 census to establish a person's age. (Census Search/10/478, return for Co. Fermanagh, Barony of Magheraboy, Parish of Inishmacsaint, Townland of Killy More.)

SUBSEQUENT POLITICAL HISTORY

The history of the Irish Free State and Northern Ireland after 1922 is rather complicated. After the suppression of the IRA, the Irish Free State continued its connection with Britain but had a decidedly Roman-Catholic ethos. In Northern Ireland, Protestants retained their hold on political and economic power. For a number of years, its parliament was held in Union Theological College, the Presbyterian seminary at Queen's University, until a new parliament building was built on the Stormont Estate in east Belfast. Not only did "two solitudes" exist between the two counties, but also between the Catholic and Protestant residents of each country.

The Irish Free State moved into a more republican stance in 1937, when it adopted a new constitution and called itself Éire, replacing the British governor general with an Irish president. Éire soon withdrew from Britain's military sphere by closing its harbours to the Royal Navy and remaining neutral during the Second World War.

In November 1948, the prime minister of Éire, while visiting Canada, announced the withdrawal of Éire from the British Commonwealth. Éire officially declared itself the Republic of Ireland, which really legalized the *de facto* situation that had existed since 1937. Britain accepted this reality in 1949.

The events in the Republic increased the mistrust and militant attitudes that Protestants in Northern Ireland had toward the Republic and Catholics. Economic inequality experienced by Catholics in both counties led to the revival of the IRA in the 1960s. This, in turn, led to the "Troubles" in Northern Ireland — a thirty-year civil war, which resulted in up to five thousand people dying from assassinations, paramilitary battles, and conflicts with British forces.

During this terrible period, there were some bright lights who sought to bring peace to the "two solitudes." Among them were two clergymen in Belfast: the Reverend Ken Newell and Father Gerry Reynolds, respectively Presbyterian and Roman Catholic, whose deep friendship and Christian commitment caused them bring their congregations together in joint services. Together, they reached out to those who were suffering during the conflict, eventually bringing together the leaders of the opposing sides in private talks. This set the stage for the peace negotiations that resulted in the Easter Accord of 1998. For their efforts, Newell and Reynolds were awarded an international mini Noble Peace Prize.

Following the peace accord, the atmosphere in both Irelands has remarkably changed. There are no longer border checkpoints. Travel between the two counties has increased, and intra-Irish tourism is encouraged. With the reduction of tensions, there has been a cultural revival that has seen a greater interest in genealogy. Catholics and Protestants are now working together in genealogical and family history societies, thus helping to break down former barriers.

While many of Ireland's documentary records have been lost, let no one tell you that there are no Irish records. We have listed many that are still held in Irish archives, but there are many more which exist in England, Scotland, and the countries to which your ancestors moved. Concerted detective work will help you solve the mystery of the origins of your Irish ancestors. The next chapter will show you how to do it.

CHAPTER TWO

Finding Clues to the County in Ireland

The success of any genealogical quest for information on our Irish ancestors depends on the amount of research that we do in the country to which they immigrated, whether it be the Antipodes (Australia and New Zealand), Canada, or the United States. This means considerable homework before we even think of going to Ireland to find our ancestors. It requires a systematic investigative approach to sleuth out the Irish county of origin. You will have to use traditional research techniques and Internet sources, neither of which can be ignored.

We need to examine the paper trail that our ancestors left in their new country. And do not forget the collateral family lines! The records of siblings, aunts, uncles — and great-aunts and great-uncles — may contain the information that we need. Richard Doherty of Celtic Quest spent thirteen years trying to locate the Irish county from which his family came. By accident he found in the nursing home application of one of his relatives that his family had been born in County Kerry. Once he had that information, Richard was able to search the records of one county rather than thirty-two.

In addition to collateral family lines, one should also remember that people sometimes came in groups and settled together.

Neighbours' documents may help you locate the Irish county in question.

ORAL TRADITIONS

It is wise to start with what your family knows about its past. An elderly relative may have information — even a name of a county, townland, or parish — from where your family came. These leads need to be followed. They may possess postcards or letters sent by family members who stayed behind in Ireland.

FAMILY BIBLES

Family Bibles sometimes contain detailed information in the baptism, marriage, and death section. This is a start, but we must be careful not to take the information as gospel, because it may not have been recorded at the time of the events, especially if the penmanship and the ink are all the same.

This Methodist baptismal certificate, held by my client's family, included the townland, location of the church, county, and name of the parents. It made searching their family's genealogy rather easy.

Sometimes family Bibles were used as repositories for family treasures. Tucked between the pages, you may find baptismal certificates, marriage licenses, communion cards, obituaries, and funeral cards. It was the documents that I found in my grandmother's Bible that started me on my heritage quest.

LOCAL HISTORIES AND HISTORICAL ATLASES

Local histories can often provide you with information about the origin of your Irish ancestors. In Ontario, Canada, the historical atlases that were published in the late 1800s are even more detailed, and they could contain biographies of the subscribers. I discovered a portrait of my great grandmother's brother and an extensive write-up on him in the *Huron County Historical Atlas*, which stated that he was born in County Fermanagh.

In the late 1800s, the Chicago company Goodspeed Publishing produced many county histories. Usually, the Goodspeed name appeared in the title of these histories. Similar publications were prepared for some counties in Ontario, and all of these texts are filled with biographical information.

Similarly, a competitor in Chicago — Warner, Beers & Company — produced county histories around the United States. They also came into Canada and created *Beer's Commemorative Biographical Records* for some of the counties of western Ontario. Subscribers usually wrote their own entries; they are worth investigating.

One should not forget the family histories that were published by the Women's Institutes. In Canada they were called *Tweedsmuir Histories*, after Lady Tweedsmuir, who was a patron of the organization, her husband being Lord Tweedsmuir, governor general of Canada. The *Tweedsmuir Histories* cover houses, farms, family histories, and genealogies, and the Ontario Genealogical Society is in the process of digitizing these texts.

younger days, but later in life became superintendent of a Cotton Manufacturing Company.

On April 7, 1892, Thomas King was married to Victorie Dolsen, and one child was born of this union, Elma J. Mrs. King was born in Raleigh township on the old Dolsen homestead, June 1, 1861, daughter of Daniel and Jane (Morden) Dolsen, of Raleigh township, and near London, Ont., respectively. They died at St. Johns, he in 1883, aged sixty years, and she in 1880.

Mr. King remained on the farm until he was eleven years old, when he went to the village of Dundas, Ont., and there attended school. In 1876 he went to Dresden, Ont., and continued his attendance at school until he was eighteen. He then learned the machinist's trade, which he has followed ever since. In 1884 he left St. Thomas, where he had followed his trade for a year, and went to Chatham, but after a year more he went to Montana, spent another year, and tried Atlantic, Iowa, for a few months, thence going to Omaha, Nebraska. After a few months in that city, he returned to Dresden, and soon thereafter bought his present property, as mentioned above. In politics, he is a Reformer, and has served as township councillor for a year. Fraternally, he belongs to the I. O. O. F. and Encampment, and he attends and subscribes to the Presbyterian Church. Mr. King is naturally considered one of the leading men of Dresden, and he has a host of friends not only there, but throughout the county.

FATHER MICHAEL JOSEPH BRADY is pastor of one of the finest Roman Catholic churches in Ontario. He came from St. Alphonsus Church, at Windsor, on Jan. 13, 1899, to take charge of the parish of Wallaceburg, and much of the growth and development of this parish is directly due to his excellent business management and persevering energy. The fine church which now stands as a memorial of religious zeal on the part of the Wallaceburg parish replaces a wooden structure erected in 1862, the same now being used as a school building. A brick structure was completed in 1878, and it was visited at monthly intervals by a priest from Chatham. The first regular resident priest was Father James Ryan, who served from 1879 to 1887, and he was followed by

Father John Rolan, who served for fourteen years and was succeeded by Father Brady. The parochial residence (costing $10,000) was opened May 6, 1902. The church and residence adjoining have been fitted with all modern conveniences, and the people of the Wallaceburg parish have every reason to feel proud of their church, their parish house and their scholarly and devoted priest.

Father Brady was born Oct. 29, 1862, at St. Thomas, Ont., son of Patrick and Mary (Doyle) Brady, natives of County Wexford, Ireland, the former of whom came to Canada in 1824. They were married in St. Thomas, Ont. Mr. Brady took up 200 acres of land in Yarmouth township, County of Elgin, which is still in the possession of the family, although it is worked by others, and he was a successful farmer, a quiet, moral man who devoted his life to agricultural pursuits and the welfare of his family. His death occurred Oct. 9, 1889, at the age of seventy-six years. Some idea of the esteem in which he was held may be gathered from the fact that 100 carriages followed his remains to the beautiful Catholic cemetery at St. Thomas, where a fine monument of Scotch granite marks the last resting place of him and his devoted wife, who died in 1867, aged thirty-five years. Their children were: Thomas, who died aged thirty-nine years, was engaged in a real estate business; James, a miner at Cripple Creek, Colorado; John, a prominent man in Chicago, Illinois, the inventor of the Brady Steam Turbine engine; Father Michael J.; Martin, who died aged nineteen years; Mary, who was Mother Superior of the Convent of the Sacred Heart at London, Ont., and died in 1884; Margaret, who married Cornelius Coughlin, and died in New York City, leaving three children, one of whom is our subject's capable housekeeper; and Anna, who died in 1894, aged forty-one years, having resided with her brother in Chicago for a number of years.

After completing his elementary education in the schools of his native town, Father Brady completed his classical, philosophical and theological courses at St. Michael's College at Toronto, and the Grand Seminary University at Montreal, when he was ordained a priest by the late distinguished Archbishop Walsh, on Dec. 8, 1884, at the Sacred Heart Convent at London, Ont., his sister being at that time assistant Mother Superior. His earliest days in

Commemorative Biographical Record for the County of Kent, Ontario. (1904.) Many times, these volumes contain information that point to the county of Irish origin, but we must also be careful about the factual information provided. In this case, most of the dates for Father Brady were inaccurate.

CENSUS RESEARCH

In most genealogical investigations, we automatically go to the census records of the country to which our ancestors came. Most of us have found that their census returns simply state "Ireland." However, some census takers in the 1851 and 1861 Canadian census actually listed the Irish county of origin.

One also needs to remember that the Irish sometimes spent some time in England or Scotland before moving on, and the associated census returns from 1871 onward might contain their Irish county of birth. If they had children born in Scotland, the

A portion of the 1881 British census. After 1871 the British census gave the county of birth for those Irish living in Britain. The highlighted section indicates that Caroline was born in County Cork.

PERSONAL CENSUS—ENUMERATION DISTRICT, No. _five_ _____ 51 OF

	Names of Inmates.	Profession, Trade or Occupation.	Place of Birth.	Religion.	Residence if out of limits.	Age next birth day.	Male.	Female.
	1	2	3	4	5	6	7	8
1	Eliza Miller		Fitzroy C.W.	Methodist	Fitzroy	6		1
2	Abraham Miller		Do	Do	Do	4	1	
3	Elvina Miller		Do	Do	Do	3		1
4	William Miller		Do	Do	Do	1	1	B
5	Cuth' Martin	Servant	Cavan Ireland	Roman Catholic		16	1	
6	Nath' Rowan	Labourer	Mayo Ireland	Do		34	1	
7	Ann Rowan		Do	Do		30		1
8	Francis Rowan		Do	Do	Do	12	1	
9	Cath' Rowan		Do	Do	Do	10		1
10	John Rowan		Do	Do	Do	8	1	
11	Margaret Rowan		Fitzroy C.W.	Do	Do	6		1
12	Arthur Rowan		Do	Do	Do	4	1	
13	Nath' Rowan		Do	Do	Do	2	1	
14	Mich' Rowan		Do	Do	Do	1	1	B
15	David Elliott	Farmer	Cavan Ireland	Methodist	Do	74	1	
16	Martha Elliott		Do	Do	Do	64		1
17	John Elliott	Labourer	Do	Do	Do	25	1	
18	Eliza Elliott		Do	Do	Do	23	1	
19	Thomas Elliott	Labourer	Do	Do	Do	23	1	
20	Mich' Costello	Do	Tipperary	Do	Do	20	1	
21	Mich' Costello	Do	Do	Do	Do	50	1	
22	Mary Costello		Do	Do	Do	45		1
23	Ann Costello		Do	Do	Do	21		1
24	John Costello		Do	Do	Do	17	1	
25	Will' Wilson	Farmer	Mayo Ireland	Do	Do	40	1	
26	Eliza Wilson		Do	Do	Do	36		1
27	John Wilson	Labourer	Fitzroy C.W.	Do	Do	19	1	
28	William Wilson		Do	Do	Do	17	1	
29	James Wilson		Do	Do	Do	15	1	
30	Jane Wilson		Do	Do	Do			1
31	Ellen Wilson		Do	Do	Do	12		1
32	Alexander Wilson		Do	Do	Do	10	1	
33	Rachel Wilson		Do	Do	Do	6		1
34	Eliza Wilson		Do	Do	Do	5		1
35	Rich' Wilson		Do	Do	Do	1	1	B
36	Patrick Jeffery	Farmer	Down Ireland	Church of Scotland	Do	56	1	
37	Agnes Jeffery		Do	Do	Do	29		1
38	John Jeffery	Labourer	Do	Do	Do	18	1	
39	James Jeffery		Do	Do	Do	15	1	
40	James Elliott	Farmer (Spinster)	Mayo Ireland	Church of England	Do	71	1	
41	Cuth' Elliott		Do	Do	Do	53		1
42	Geo G. Elliott		Sligo	Do	Do	15	1	
43	Mary Elliott		Mayo Ireland	Do	Do	30		1
44	Margaret Elliott		Tipperary	Do	Do	25		1
45	Matilda Elliott		Sligo England	Do	Do	19		1
46	Eliza Elliott		Cork Ireland	Do	Do	13		1
47	Cath' Elliott		Do	Do	Do	7		1
48	James Brown	Farmer	Cavan Ireland	Do	Do	37	1	
49	Isabella Brown		Do	Do	Do	32		1
50	Martha Brown		Do	Do	Do	11		1
						25	25	

1851 Canada West Census for Fitzroy Township. This enumerator included the county of origin in Ireland, making the genealogist's job easier.

birth certificates issued 1855 contained the date and place of marriage of the parents — another possible avenue to finding their county in Ireland.

In the North American censuses, you may see that some of the family members were married in Ireland before they came to the new host country, because they had children born in Ireland. If they were married after 1845 (if Protestants, or after 1864 for Catholics), their Irish marriage registration, which can be located on *www.familysearch.org*, will give their county. If they had children born after 1864 in Ireland, their birth registrations will be useful. All you have to do is to order the certificates from the General Register Office in Ireland or Northern Ireland, and the certificates will give you the county, parish, and townland of the people you are seeking.

MARRIAGE RECORDS

Depending on the time and place of marriage, records sometimes contained the county or parish of birth in Ireland. If a second marriage took place, the registration might contain even more specific information than the first, because more was asked of the couple. Again, look at the marriage records of siblings.

Many of the Canadian marriage records are indexed by the provincial governments or, in the case of the U.S. records, the state governments. While the searching is usually free, to see actual copies you might have to pay-per-view or order by mail. Some are available on *www.ancestry.com*, which can be used at most public libraries if you do not have your own subscription.

Birth, marriage, and death records from New South Wales, Australia, have been indexed from 1788 and are available online from the State Archives. To view the records, you will have to pay online. Visit *www.bdm.nsw.gov.au/familyHistory/searchHistorical Records.htm*.

Left: *Ontario marriage registration, 1870 (RG 80-5-0-3 v.2/3 p.79, 1 March 1870, MS 932 reel 1). Both spouses listed County Tyrone as their birthplace.*

Below: *Ontario death registration, 1887 (RG 80-8-0-117 v.C p.121, 7204/1887, MS 935, reel 47). It gives his birthplace as Fivemiletown, County Tyrone.*

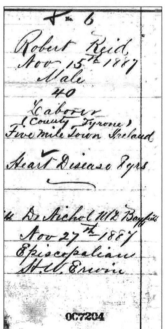

DOCUMENTS RELATING TO DEATH

Sometimes, exact information on place of birth can be found on death certificates. This information is only as good as the knowledge of informant who supplied it to the registrar of deaths. How many of us know the birth information of our mother-in-law and her parents?

Besides death certificates, there are a host of other documents relating to death that might reveal genealogical clues: township burial authorizations, church burial registers, funeral home records, and funeral cards. Various genealogical societies are now collecting

Newmarket Cemetery Company burial ledger. Lines 1063 and 1069 gave county of birth in Ireland.

and indexing funeral home cards, because they sometimes contain detailed information on place of birth. I have found that the amount of information on Michigan county and state death registrations is quite different — both records should be checked.

Newspaper obituaries are also good sources of information, but be sure to go beyond the death notice to see if a full obituary is given. They sometimes appear before or after the funeral, so check the papers even a week or two after the death. Also, check other newspapers if more than one served the area.

Even though many people left Ireland in distress, they held their place of birth in high regard and sometimes included their county, parish, and even townland on their tombstones, which is another good avenue to explore.

Death of Daniel Phelan.

Mr. Daniel Phelan passed away at his apartments in the O'Neill House, at 7.10 o'clock this morning. Old age and failing health had been telling on him for some time past and for over two months he has been confined to his bed. Death therefore was not unexpected, but was the natural culmination of a gradual decline.

Mr. Phelan was one of Woodstock's oldest citizens; he was born in Athy, Ireland, and came to Woodstock with his father about 55 years ago. He was engaged with his father for many years in a general store business. He subsequently engaged in business in Ingersoll and while there was fortunate in acquiring considerable of the world's goods.

Obituary, Woodstock Sentinal Review, *15 August 1891, p. 4. Not only was the county of Ireland given, but also the town.*

Clifford Cemetery, Huron County, Ontario. Note that the town and county are listed on the headstone.

They say that "where there is a will, there are relatives." Probated wills often reveal considerable genealogical information. There may be references to property back in Ireland or bequests to family members still there. Sometimes, quitclaims, in which beneficiaries declined an interest in the estate, reveal locations of family members.

LAND RECORDS

In Lower and Upper Canada, land grants were issued to retired members of the British Army or Royal Navy; the Irish were well represented in the British forces. In their petitions to the Crown for these land grants, veterans often provided their military history and regimental unit. Indexes to the Upper and Lower

Canada Land Petitions are available on the Library and Archives Canada site: *www.collectionscanada.gc.ca.*

An index to the Upper Canada Land petitions has also been published by the Ontario Genealogical Society. The actual petitions have been microfilmed and are available in most research libraries, and there is a plan to digitize these documents.

These land petitions can contain information on the birthplace of the applicant. Sometimes the petition was made while the person was still in Ireland, and the return address on the correspondence may provide the clue you need.

With the name of your ancestor's regimental unit, it may be possible to locate his military service records. The site *www. findmypast.co.uk* allows access to digitized images of the discharge papers of Chelsea pensioners from 1760 to 1913, for over a million veterans. Some files contain attestation papers, which were signed when joining up, and these provide their place of birth.

Another type of land grant system in Canada involved western Land Grants, made available to immigrants from 1870 to 1930. These land grants were situated in Western Canada and can be searched on *www.collectionscanada.gc.ca.* The actual files can be obtained from the various provincial archives in Western Canada. Sometimes, these files have detailed information on the family, including genealogical details. Some files still contain the Application for Entry for a Homestead forms that asked the claimant his or her country and county of birth.

Land grants were also awarded to military personnel in Australia and Tasmania as Aborigines were driven off of their traditional lands. You may find your Irish ancestors' county of origin in those records, which are available through the State Archives of New South Wales.

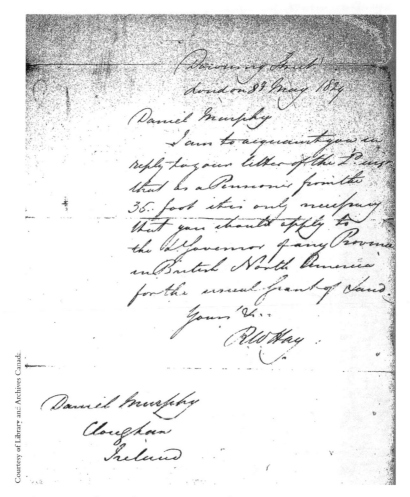

Upper Canada Land Petitions. Letter from R. W. Hay, Government Offices, Downing Street, London, to Daniel Murphy, Cloghan, Ireland. (Executive Council of the Province of Upper Canada fonds, Vol. 353, Bundle M16, Petition 163, Microfilm C-2210.) A brief search revealed that Cloghan was in Gallen Parish, King's County (Offaly).

Chelsea Pensioner Military Record for Daniel Murphy. This shows that Daniel Murphy was born in Gallen Parish, King's County, and signed up at Strabane, County Londonderry. Strabane was actually in County Tyrone.

OTHER BRITISH RECORDS

At one time, it was said that the sun never set on the British Empire. British troops and consular officials served around the globe. Sometimes, they married women in the country in which they served and even had children there; others may have died during their tour of duty. Much of this information is available, as British military chaplains recorded the marriages, baptisms, and burials they performed. Consular activities and chaplains' records have

Courtesy of the GRO, England

British military chaplains' baptism returns from across the empire. Using the reference numbers, you can order the certificates from the GRO, England. They often predate civil registrations.

An Entry in the Army Register **CERTIFIED COPY OF** **AN ENTRY OF** BIRTH **SA** 077428
Book of Births, Baptisms and Marriages

Application Number....224

Registration of Births, Deaths and | | **Marriages (Special Provisions) Act 1957**

South Mayo Regiment of Militia

Date of the Child's Birth	Place and Date of the Child's Baptism Place	Date	Christian Name of the Child	Parents' Names Christian	Surname	Rank of the Father	Name of the Chaplain or other Clergyman by whom the ceremony was performed
30 June 1859	Curragh Camp	20 July 1859	Lilly	George & Lilly	Taylor	Qr. Mr. Sergt.	Revd. A. Henderson Army Chaplain

No. 57   I certify the above Registry to be correct

Signature of the Adjutant J.V. Whaite Capt.

CERTIFIED to be a true copy of ~~the certified copy of~~ an entry made in a Service Departments Register.
Given at the GENERAL REGISTER OFFICE, under the Seal of the said Office, the   **12th**   day of   **April 2010**

If the certificate is given from the original register the words "the certified copy of" are struck out. Section 3(2) of the above mentioned Act provides that "The enactments relating to the registration of births and deaths and marriages in England and Wales, Scotland and Northern Ireland (which contain provisions authorising the admission in evidence of, and of extracts from, certified copies of registers and duplicate registers) shall have effect as if the Service Departments Registers were certified copies or duplicate registers transmitted to the Registrar General in accordance with these enactments."

CAUTION: THERE ARE OFFENCES RELATING TO FALSIFYING OR ALTERING A CERTIFICATE AND USING OR POSSESSING A FALSE CERTIFICATE
©CROWN COPYRIGHT
WARNING: A CERTIFICATE IS NOT EVIDENCE OF IDENTITY.

Courtesy of the GRO, England.

An example of a military baptism certificate, County Kildare, 1859.

been collected and are indexed on *www.findmypast.co.uk* according to name, place, regiment, and the reference numbers. Copies of these records can be obtained from the General Register office in England at *www.gro.gov.uk/gro/content/certificates/default.asp*.

Using this database, I was able to obtain a registration of a military marriage of an Irishman that took place on an island off Gibraltar in 1814, as well as several baptisms of children of soldiers done in Dublin and County Kildare long before civil registration in Ireland.

UNITED STATES MILITARY RECORDS

Irish who had settled in the United States served in the armed forces during the Revolutionary and the Civil Wars and performed other military service. Many U.S. military collections have been indexed, and some are digitized and can be found on *www.ancestry.com*. You may find your Irish ancestors in these records, and even if you cannot find their attestation papers online, you may find references to the complete service records, which may lead you to their place of birth.

CANADIAN MILITARY RECORDS

Your Irish ancestor may have served in the Boer War or First World War. While some Irish came to Canada and served with the Canadian forces, their next of kin may have remained in Ireland, and their attestation papers might give information on where they lived. The military attestation papers can be found at *www.collectionscanada.gc.ca*.

PASSENGER LISTS AND IMMIGRATION RECORDS

Immigrants to North America, especially those escaping the Irish famine, landed at whatever port they could find, either in Canada or the United States, then travelled on to their destinations. Passenger lists for those entering ports on the Eastern Seaboard of the United States date from 1800. Other immigrants entered the United States through New Orleans and travelled inland up the Mississippi River. While some passenger lists gave only the point of departure, others recorded their last place of residence. These can be found on *www.ancestry.com*. Occasionally, the ship lists — particularly those for the J. & J. Cooke Line — included the town or townland of the passengers.

Some Irish who had settled travelled to North America via Glasgow or Liverpool. Formerly engaged in the slave trade, Liverpool was a transportation hub. You will also find Irish leaving from their own ports, including Belfast, Dublin, New Ross, Cork, Limerick, Sligo, and Londonderry, among others.

An 1818 passenger list from Philadelphia that gave Irish address of origin. Note highlighted section where Omagh is indicated.

Castle Garden, a former military battery, was the immigration station at New York City from 1855 to 1891. It was succeeded by Ellis Island in 1892. Its surviving immigration records are available free on *www.ellisisland.org*. Another site, *http://stevemorse.org*, has a powerful search engine for both the Castle Garden and Ellis Island records.

Canada did not regularly keep passenger lists until 1865, although there are some from earlier. Its main ports were Halifax, Saint John, and Quebec City. Some of the early passenger records can be found on *www.ingeneas.com.* The post-1865 arriving passenger lists are available on the Library and Archives Canada site, *www. collectionscanada.gc.ca.* Canadian immigration papers from 1919 to 1924 have been digitized and are available on *www.ancestry.com.*

Another source of passenger information are the records of the quarantine station at Grosse Île in the Saint Lawrence River, east of Quebec City. It was established in 1832 because of the cholera epidemic that Irish immigrants had brought to Canada. The database, also available at *www.collectionscanada.gc.ca,* lists the names of those who had been buried at sea — or quarantined or died at Grosse Île from 1832 to 1937. Occasionally, the counties of the deceased were given and the names of surviving family members were listed.

IRISH CONVICTS

During the eighteenth and nineteenth centuries, the British government sent Irish convicts to North America (until the American Revolutionary War) and Australia to remove troublemakers and relieve pressure on existing prison facilities. Their crimes ranged from stealing food in order to survive to taking part in civil rebellions. The National Archives of Ireland has indexed the transportation records of these Irish convicts, and the databases contain information on their names, age, crime, year and place of trial, and sentence; visit *www.nationalarchives.ie* for this information. See also *http://members.pcug.org.au/~ppmay/convicts.htm* for a list of convicts sent to New South Wales. It includes not only the above information, but also their native county and occupation.

Not only convicts settled in Australia. Sometimes, family members of convicts chose to follow them to Australia. Some wanting a warmer climate went there on their own, while still others had some form of government assistance. The gold rush in Australia from 1851 to 1871 also attracted adventurers. You may find their county of origin in the records held by the State Archives of New South Wales.

POOR HOUSE OR HOSPITAL RECORDS

Sometimes, when Irish immigrants landed, they were destitute or ill and had to be put in local hospitals or poor houses. Such people who arrived in Saint John, New Brunswick, between 1841 and 1849 have been indexed. Their information usually included their county in Ireland. These records can be found on *www.ancestry.com*.

IMMIGRATION AID SOCIETIES

In many port cities, immigration aid societies were established to help poor immigrants get to their place of destination. The records for one such agency in Montreal from 1832 listed names, county of origin, occupation, number in the family, and where they were sent. These digitized records are found at *www.collectionscanada.gc.ca*. You should look for similar record collections from other port cities through which your families passed.

HOME CHILDREN

Various agencies sprang up in Great Britain to aid children who were orphans or waifs. The most famous are the Dr. Barnardo Homes. Others organizations were the Salvation Army, Fegan Homes, MacPherson Homes, and various Catholic bodies. Between 1869 and 1930, over one hundred thousand children from England, Ireland, and Scotland were sent to Canada to work on farms or as domestics. Some of them were abused and exploited in their new settings. Indeed, many of these children were not orphans, but had been removed from their parents for the purpose of social engineering.

Information on these home children arrivals in Canada is available on the Library and Archives Canada website, *www.collectionscanada.gc.ca*. From the information given, you may be able to obtain the complete files of your home-child ancestor from the agencies that sent them to Canada. The Dr. Barnardo Homes have become quite responsive to requests for information.

NATURALIZATION RECORDS

Irish immigrants in the United States often took out American citizenship. One should check their naturalization files to look for information on their county of birth. Those Irish who came to Canada did not have to undergo naturalization, because they were already British subjects.

U.S.–CANADA BORDER CROSSINGS

In the nineteenth century, there was considerable movement back and forth across the U.S.–Canadian border, almost as if there were no border. In 1895 the U.S. government began keeping track of border crossings. Those records have been digitized from that date until 1956 and are available on *www.ancestry.com*. Another set of records exists for crossings at Detroit and Port Huron, dating from 1905 to 1957, and entries from Mexico for the period 1895 to 1957. Some of those documents cover two pages, so it is important to click on the "next" button to see all of the information. The specific place of birth is often given.

Similarly, the Canadian government began keeping border entries from 1908. Those digitized records, also on *www.ancestry.com*

An example of a US–Canada border entry card, giving Tipperary as county of birth.

and *collectionscanada.gc.ca*, extend to 1935. Information on British subjects entering Canada was included on the Form 30A, used from 1919 to 1924. You might find your Irish ancestor's county of birth listed in those records.

IMMIGRANT SAVINGS BANKS

Various agencies were established to help Irish immigrants send money back home to family members during the famine or to pay for their passage to North America. One such agency was the New York Emigrant Savings Bank, which opened in 1850 and operated until 1883. Its digitized records provide information on the account holders: their New York address, date of arrival and ship name, birthplace, and the names of their relatives back in the old country. These records can be accessed on *www.ancestry.com* in the U.S. immigration section.

A sample of an Emigrant Savings Bank test book page.

The Canada Company had a similar banking service. Record books of remittances to family members back in the British Isles contain the names of the senders as well as the names and addresses of the recipients. These records are at the Archives of Ontario, and an index of the recipients has been made.

U.S. PASSPORTS

The U.S. government has issued passports since 1795, and *www.ancestry.com* has indexed and digitized them up to 1925. In the passport applications, you can find the detailed place of birth and information on parents and their birthplace.

Courtesy of National Archives, Washington, D.C., and www.ancestry.com.

U.S. passport application indicating the person was born in County Cavan on 15 May 1830.

U.S. SOCIAL SECURITY DEATH INDEX

In 1937 the U.S. government instituted its social security system. After that time, people had to apply, and their applications might include their place of birth in Ireland. After the people's deaths, they were entered on the Social Security Death Index, which can be accessed on *www.ancestry.com*. It will generate a form for you to send to the appropriate government department in order to get a copy of the person's original social security application.

MISSING PERSONS NEWSPAPER ADS

Sometimes families back in Ireland lost touch with children or spouses who had moved to Australia or North America. They might have put an advertisement in newspapers looking for them. The *Irish Canadian*, based in Toronto, often carried such ads. So did other major newspapers in Canada and the United States. You might check online newspaper collections available through *www.ancestry.com*, Paper of Record, the *Toronto Star's*

Courtesy of Paper of Record.

An ad placed in the Irish Canadian *of Toronto, 2 November 1864.*

Pages of the Past, and World Vital Records, which have powerful search engines. From the ads, you may not only find the county of origin, but also the names of other family members.

ORANGE LODGES

Some of our Irish ancestors may have belonged to the militant Protestant Orange Order, either in Ireland or in their adopted country. Lodge membership applications usually included the county of birth. If a person transferred his lodge membership from an Irish lodge, you may find out where he was living in Ireland. Susan Smart of the York Branch of the Ontario Genealogical Society has produced a CD of Orange Lodge records that were found in an attic in York County, Ontario. You should search out the person's last Orange Lodge membership and work back through earlier memberships.

Orange Lodge transfer certificate from County Armagh.

MASONIC LODGES

Many Irish Protestants also belonged to Masonic Lodges, and may also have transferred their membership from Ireland. As before, start with the local lodge and work back to the beginning of their membership. The Masonic headquarters on Molesworth Street in Dublin, about a block from the National Library, has a database of its membership after 1870, but also has membership files for prior to that date.

If your detective work in the sources of the adopted country of your Irish ancestor has not yielded his or her native county in Ireland, the following computerized sources may help you locate the clues you are looking for.

COMPREHENSIVE COMPUTERIZED SEARCHES

Since the indexing and digitization of many Irish records, it is now possible to search the entire island of Ireland for your ancestors. Some of these searches are available free of charge, while others are pay-per-view or subscription sites.

Flax Growers Bounty, 1796

The production of linen out of flax was a very important industry in Ireland and occupied the lives of many people. In order to stimulate the industry, the Irish Linen Board offered free spinning wheels and looms depending on how many acres of flax were grown. Information was kept on almost sixty thousand Irish who received this benefit. Their names, counties, and parishes can be searched on many of the Irish websites.

Tithe Applotments

Recently, *www.ancestry.com* has added tithe applotment records to its Irish site, but the collection is not complete. If your ancestor leased farmland between 1821 and 1838, you may find him or her in these records. Remember, only the head of the household was listed. You can only get the index at this point. If you want copies of the original tithe documents, the microfilms can be obtained from the Latter Day Saints (Mormons). Lists of tithe defaulters in the southern counties have also been put online at *www.irishorigins.com* and *www.findmypast.ie*.

Searching Surviving 1841 and 1851 Abstracts

On *www.ireland-genealogy.com*, it is now possible to search, for free, the surviving copies of the 1841 and 1851 census forms that were used to support applications for the 1908 old-age pension program. An advanced-search feature will allow you to search the entire island. If you want to see extracts of the documents, you can pay £2 to see each one.

Griffith's Valuation

The *Griffith's Primary Valuation* was done between 1848 and 1862, depending on the county. It only listed the heads of the households on the townlands. It is free to search on *http://askaboutireland.ie/ griffith-valuation/index.xml*, and you can also download the images.

Belfast Burial Records

Within the past year, the Belfast City Council has placed the burial records for many of its cemeteries online. The site has a powerful search engine and it provides the name, last address, age, date of death, date of burial, cemetery, grave section and number, and type of burial. This is a free site. Visit it at *www.belfastcity.gov. uk/burialrecords/search.asp*. You might find your elusive ancestor by this means.

Royal Irish Constabulary

Between 1816 and 1922, many Irish men joined the Royal Irish Constabulary (RIC), the paramilitary force in Ireland. Its members were different from the British bobbies in that they were armed and were posted to counties outside of where they were born.

Name SYDNEY SMITH

Rank Sub Constable

Number 1055

Age on Joining 21 years	*Height* 5 ft 7 in	

Religion P.   *D.O.B.*

Date of Appointment May 1831

Native County Queens

Recommended By J. Tabuteau Esq.

Trade Calling weaver

Date of Discharge/Dismissed/Resign/Death   Pensioned
15.9.1851 @
£16 per annum

Allocated to / Transfers Clare (10 years), Tipperary (North Riding)

Promotions

Awards

Punishments

Injuries

Date Married November 1837

Native County Of Wife Clare

A Royal Irish Constabulary service record extract. The document gives Sydney Smith's birthplace (Queen's County) as well as his wife's (County Clare). It also notes his prior occupation, his sponsor, his date of marriage, and where he served.

Almost seventy thousand service records have been indexed on *www.ancestry.com* and elsewhere. After finding an RIC member in the index, you can obtain an extract of his service record from the Police Service of Northern Ireland museum. It will give you his year and county of birth, the name of his sponsor, his prior occupation, when and where marriages occurred, the birthplace of wife, the places he served, and when he left the RIC service. The extract costs £25, and more for those above the rank of Sergeant. See *www.psni.police.uk/index/about-us/police_museum/museum_genealogy.htm*.

Dublin Metropolitan Police

The Dublin Metropolitan Police (DMP) was formed in 1836 and modelled after the London Metropolitan Police Force. It existed until 1925 and employed over twelve thousand men. Jim Herlihy has written a short history of the force, and it includes a genealogical guide on searching the DMP employment records.

London Metropolitan Police

Many Irish joined the London Metropolitan Police. The National Archives of England has information on obtaining their service records, but has not yet listed their names on its site.

Irish Family History Foundation

For many years, county heritage societies have existed in Ireland. They had collected information from church registers and cemeteries, but the societies were not very genealogically friendly. Around 2005, many of these county organizations came under the umbrella of the Irish Family History Foundation, which has created a large database of those records — with the exception of those from Counties Clare, Kerry, South Cork,

Waterford, Wexford, Carlow, and Dublin city. Visit it at *www. rootsireland.ie/ifhf.*

These records are not complete, but you may be able to find your ancestors in the database. You can search by individual county or the entire database, which contains over eighteen million records. There are advanced searching features, but it is still a fishing expedition and can be expensive. You can do your searches free, but if you wish to see an extract of the document, you must buy credits. Each view costs €5.

PRONI

The Public Record Office of Northern Ireland in Belfast has an ever-expanding database of indexes and digitized documents, which might help you locate that elusive Irish ancestor. This includes its digitized card catalogue of names, wills, freeholder's lists, city directories, and signers of the Ulster Covenant. This is a free website and can be found at *www.proni.gov.uk.*

www.irishgenealogy.ie

This site, operated by the Irish Department of Tourism, Culture and Sport, has indexed over two million of Church of Ireland records for Counties Cork, Kerry, Carlow, and the city of Dublin. Many digital images of the records are available on the site. Sometimes, church ceremonies were performed for people from outside these counties, and the search engine can pick them up if you search by their home county. Visit *www.irishgenealogy.ie.*

Emerald Ancestors

Emerald Ancestors is a subscription site that offers access to its database of over one million names from a limited number of church registers, civil registrations, graveyards, and census data. It specializes in Northern Ireland and the counties of historic

Ulster. You can do an initial free search, but it if want to see the details, you must purchase a subscription for one month, half a year, or for the whole year. Visit *www.emeraldancestors.com*.

Ulster Historical Foundation

Based in Belfast, the Ulster Historical Foundation operates a genealogical research centre and a large database of church records for Counties Antrim and Down. You can do an initial search for free and continue on a pay-per-view basis if you want to see the abstracts of those records.

The foundation also offers a guild membership that gives you access to its database of many other records. Their linked site, History from Headstones, has transcriptions of many cemetery tombstones. While its focus is on the current counties of Northern Ireland, there are also documents in the database pertaining to other parts of the country. Members also get a reduced rate when accessing the abstracts of the church records. Visit *www. ancestryireland.com*.

www.findmypast.ie

The newest online genealogy collection for Ireland is *www. findmypast.ie*, a co-operative effort of the British site Findmypast and Eneclann in Dublin. It is a pay-per-view or subscription database that contains various vital records, census substitutes, land and estate records, court records, and prison registers, as well as migration, military, and rebellion documents.

Surnames Search

If you still have not discovered what county your ancestors came from, try another tack. Since the digitization of vast amounts of records, it is now possible to check to see where certain surnames are common. You can even search for the convergence of two different surnames. John Grenham's listings of surnames and variants are available on *www.irishtimes.com/ancestry*, which is a pay-per-view site.

Other Sources

Many Irish counties have online genealogical interest groups with impressive websites. Many of them have mounted collections of parish registers, vital records, cemetery transcriptions, census data, and other genealogical information. Members of these groups are usually quite willing to give assistance. You may find your ancestors listed in these collections. Many are hosted by Rootsweb. Google the desired county's genealogical sites.

The Ontario Genealogical Society has two special interest groups devoted to Irish Genealogy and Irish Palatines. Visit *www. ogs.on.ca/branches/branchlocator.php* for more information.

RECAPPING YOUR RESEARCH

At this point, you may have found the county of your Irish ancestors ... or possibly not. If the latter, do not despair. Look over all of your research, because you may have missed a vital clue. For ten years, I had a marriage record for one set of my great-grandparents, not realizing that it stated that he was from County Roscommon. *Check again!*

You must also remember that, of the surviving Irish records, only a fraction is online, but more are being added daily. It is wise to revisit those sites to see what is new, and more powerful search engines are also being added. Some search engines allow you to search by first name — let's hope it is not Patrick or Bridget.

Another possibility is that you might need to use alternate spellings for the names you are searching. Remember that some Irish surnames names were changed by immigration officials, and illiterate people would not have known the difference. Sometimes, people even changed their own names. The O'Neils, for example, may have become McNeils to appear more Scottish than Irish, because of anti-Irish prejudice at the time. Some may have dropped the prefixes *O'* or *Mc*, thus O'Brien or McBrien may have become Brien, Byran, or Breen.

Finally, as you research parallel family lines, or the neighbours of your ancestor, you may find the person you are looking for in the same records.

CHAPTER THREE

Zeroing in on the Parish and Townland

If you have found the Irish county where your ancestors were born, you are well on your way in your research. Now you will need to isolate the parish and, eventually, the townland, in order to find their records. In your research, it is possible that you have already discovered the county and parish of your ancestors — or you may have inadvertently stumbled across strange names that could be the names of the parish or townland but still do not know the county. This chapter will help you put these things together, using online land records such as census substitutes, parish registers, and civil registrations. First, it is important to understand the land terminology, as well as the political and religious administrative divisions of Ireland.

Ireland has had overlapping administrative borders, just like other countries. For example, in the United States and Canada, land divisions have evolved over time. Initially, there were a number of colonies and territories in North America belonging to Britain, France, or Spain that later became states or provinces, depending upon the country being formed. In 1791 Quebec was divided into Upper and Lower Canada. Upper Canada was divided into districts, and marriages were recorded according to these divisions.

In 1841 there were slight changes in the borders when Canada East and Canada West were formed, essentially matching the later provinces of Quebec and Ontario. In 1858, counties were introduced in Canada West and marriages were recorded accordingly. Each county had divisions called townships, and after 1869, vital events were recorded at the township office. In the 1970s, various Ontario townships began to be amalgamated into regional governments. For election purposes, there are also regional, provincial, and federal political ridings, but they do not match one another in area.

Similarly, Ireland has had a very complicated history of administrative borders. Below, you will find simplified information about the peculiar divisions within Ireland, which are important for genealogical research.

Provinces

Ireland was divided into five provinces: Ulster, Leinster, Meath, Munster, and Connaught, but the number was reduced to four after the Norman occupation in the twelfth century. The counties within the four provinces are often grouped together for cultural and sports purposes, but now the provinces have no legal status, except for Ulster, which is now smaller than its pre-1922 size.

Counties

There are thirty-two counties in Ireland. Since 1922, the Republic has twenty-six counties and Northern Ireland has six: Antrim, Armagh, Down, Fermanagh, Londonderry, and Tyrone. Northern Ireland is a separate country belonging to Great Britain.

For most of our genealogical research, we must forget about the 1922 border. Records generated before that time will usually be found in the archives and record offices of the Republic, although there have been record transfers and copies of documents shared between the National Archives of Ireland in Dublin

A map of the counties of Ireland and Northern Ireland.

and the Public Record Office of Northern Ireland (PRONI) in Belfast. Only since the 1922 division have generated documents been kept in their respective countries.

Parishes

Each county in Ireland was divided into a number of civil parishes, and many records are listed by this division. There were also ecclesiastical parishes. Church of Ireland (Anglican) parishes coincided with the civil parishes, because it was the state church.

Roman Catholic parishes, however, could extend beyond the civil parishes and sometimes have different names. Several reference books contain maps that show the differences between civil and Roman Catholic parishes.

When searching Roman Catholic Church registers, you need to be aware that they cover a larger area than the civil parish, but other civil documents — such as land records and census documents pertaining to those Catholics — are recorded according to the civil parish.

Diocese

A diocese is an ecclesiastical area that comprises a number of parishes and can extend over several counties, and since 1922, across the borders of Northern Ireland and the Republic. Dioceses are under the control of a bishop. Church of Ireland and Roman Catholic dioceses are different in their size.

In some cases, it is important to know the borders of each diocese. For example, Church of Ireland marriage licenses and bonds, as well as tithe applotments, were recorded at the diocesan level. If you are searching the microfilm copies of those records, you will have to keep this in mind.

Townlands

Each civil parish was divided into sections called townlands. Townlands have nothing to do with towns, but were instead very old land divisions and usually named after local geographic features. Often, their names have Gaelic roots. They could range between one to over one thousand Irish acres, which are approximately 1.6 times larger than a British acre.

Townlands are essentially rural addresses, and most documents — whether they were church register entries, land leases, censuses, or civil registrations — usually list the townland for the people mentioned. Sometimes, an unofficial local name is used on documents, which causes more confusion in identifying where people actually lived. Some local reference books can identify these alternate names of townlands.

Within Ireland and each county, you will find replication of townland names, so it is important to also know the parish to which they belonged. In 1861 a comprehensive index of townland names was made based on the 1851 census. It is called the *General Alphabetical Index to the Townlands, Towns, Parishes and Baronies of Ireland* and is the "Bible" of Irish genealogists. It names each townland and gives its size, county, barony, parish, and poor law union. It also gives its location in the 1851 census and its sheet and location on the Ordnance Survey maps. If you cannot find a copy to consult, there is an excellent website that contains much of the same information. The IreAtlas Townland Database is available at *www.seanruad.com*.

One will find that British clerics sometimes spelled the townland names phonetically and not accurately. Sometimes, the handwriting is poor. The IreAtlas Townland Database is particularly helpful in identifying the probable correct names, because it lets you sort all of the townlands within the parish. With the advanced feature, you can use the "starts with," "contains," or "ends with" sorting options. Also, you will find that the spelling of the townlands in the tithe applotments may differ from the official spelling of the names set by the 1851 census.

It is possible to see the location of townlands by searching them on Google Maps. The locations are approximate. For the Republic, you can consult the satellite images of each townland on the Environmental Protection Agency website: *http://maps.epa.ie/internetmapviewer/mapviewer.aspx*. The actual townland's size is delineated on the satellite image. In the search box, put the county and then the townland name.

ALPHABETICAL INDEX TO THE TOWNLANDS AND TOWNS OF IRELAND.

Townlands and Towns.	Area in Statute Acres. A. R. P.	County.	Barony.	Parish.	Poor Law Union in 1857.
Knocknakilly .	180 1 10	Kerry . .	Clanmaurice . .	Kilfeighny . .	Listowel .
Knocknalappa . .	345 1 1a	Clare . .	Bunratty Lower .	Kilmurry . .	Tulla . .
Knocknalear . .	87 2 35	Fermanagh .	Clankelly . .	Clones . .	Clones . .
Knocknalina . .	317 2 33	Mayo . .	Erris . .	Kilmore . .	Belmullet .
Knocknaloman . .	651 1 34	Cork, W.R.	West Muskerry .	Drishane . .	Millstreet . .
Knocknalooricaun .	356 3 33	Waterford .	Coshmore&Coshbride	Lismore and Mocollop	Lismore .
Knocknalosset . .	484 1 27	Cavan . .	Clankee . .	Knockbride . .	Cootehill .
Knocknalosset . .	236 3 30	Fermanagh .	Clankelly . .	Clones . .	Clones . .
Knocknalougha .	448 2 39	Waterford .	Coshmore&Coshbride	Lismore and Mocollop	Lismore .
Knocknalour . .	453 1 15	Wexford . .	Scarawalsh . .	Kilrush . .	Enniscorthy
Knocknalower . .	760 3 36	Mayo . .	Erris . .	Kilcommon . .	Belmullet .
Knocknalun . .	275 2 10	Monaghan .	Monaghan . .	Tedavnet . .	Monaghan .
Knocknalurgan .	124 3 27	Cork, E.R.	Kinalea . .	Carrigaline . .	Kinsale .
Knocknalyre . .	441 2 26	Cork, E.R.	Barretts . .	Garrycloyne .	Cork .
Knocknalyre .	82 3 22	Cork, E.R.	Cork . .	Ballinaboy . .	Cork .
Knocknalyre or Downhill .	60 0 37	Sligo . .	Tireragh . .	Kilmoremoy .	Ballina .
Knocknamadderee .	261 3 31	Cork, E.R.	Fermoy . .	Killathy . .	Fermoy .
Knocknamadderee .	346 3 20	Cork, E.R.	Imokilly . .	Cloyne . .	Middleton .
Knocknamaddy .	320 3 10b	Monaghan .	Cremorne . .	Ballybay . .	Castleblayney .
Knocknamallavoge .	181 1 32	Cork, E.R.	Cork . .	Inishkenny . .	Cork .
Knocknaman . .	289 1 4	Kerry . .	Magunihy . .	Kilbonane . .	Killarney .
Knocknamanagh .	595 2 31	Cork, E.R.	Kinalea . .	Tracton . .	Kinsale .
Knocknamanagh .	41 0 9	Galway . .	Dunkellin . .	Killogilleen . .	Loughrea .
Knocknamarriff .	191 3 23	Cork, E.R.	East Muskerry .	Inishcarra . .	Cork .
Knocknamarshal .	23 1 27	Wexford . .	Shelmaliere West .	Taghmon . .	Wexford .
Knocknamase or Goldengrove .	580 0 29	King's Co. .	Clonlisk . : .	Ettagh . .	Roscrea .
Knocknamaulee .	212 0 19	Waterford .	Decies without Drum	Colligan . .	Dungarvan .
Knocknambraher .	165 3 25	Queen's Co. .	Stradbally . .	Stradbally . .	Athy .
Knocknamena Commons . .	562 3 24	Tipperary, N.R.	Kilnamanagh Upper	Upperchurch .	Thurles .
Knocknamoe . .	396 3 38	Queen's Co. .	Cullenagh . .	Abbeyleix . .	Abbeyleix .
Knocknamogbalaun	196 2 27	Mayo . .	Clanmorris .	Mayo . .	Castlebar .
Knocknamohalagh .	91 2 15	Cork, W.R.	West Carbery (E.D.)	Aghadown . .	Skibbereen .
Knocknamoheragh .	372 0 36	Tipperary, N.R.	Owney and Arra	Kilnarath . .	Nenagh .
Knocknamohill .	300 0 10	Wicklow . .	Arklow . .	Castlemacadam .	Rathdrum .
Knocknamoua . .	411 1 16	Cork, E.R.	Duhallow . .	Kilshannig . .	Mallow .
Knocknamona . .	106 0 24	Donegal .	Kilmacrenan .	Conwal . .	Letterkenny .
Knocknamona . .	354 1 10	Waterford .	Decies within Drum	Ardmore . .	Dungarvan .
Knocknamota . .	261 2 6	Wexford . .	Scarawalsh . .	Carnew . .	Gorey .
Knocknamouragh .	168 3 9	Cork, E.R.	Barrymore . .	Templenacarriga	Middleton .
Knocknamuck . .	259 2 27	Cork, E.R.	Condons&Clangibbon	Brigown . .	Mitchelstown .
Knocknamuck . .	229 2 16	Cork, E.R.	Duhallow . .	Knocktemple .	Kanturk .
Knocknamuck . .	103 3 36	Cork, W.R.	Bantry . .	Kilmocomoge .	Bantry .
Knocknamuck . .	250 3 1	Kilkenny .	Crannagh . .	Tullaroan . .	Kilkenny .
Knocknamucklagh .	225 2 37	Cork, E.R.	Duhallow . .	Kilmeen . .	Kanturk .
Knocknamucklagh .	323 3 21	Kerry .	Magunihy . .	Kilnanare . .	Killarney .
Knocknamucklagh .	355 3 16	Mayo . .	Kilmaine . .	Ballinchalla . .	Ballinrobe .
Knocknamuck Lower	184 1 22	Wicklow . .	Upper Talbotstown .	Ballynure . .	Baltinglass .
Knocknamuckly .	254 1 29	Armagh . .	Oneilland East .	Seagoe . .	Lurgan .
Knocknamuck North	256 2 23	Waterford .	Coshmore&Coshbride	Lismore and Mocollop	Lismore .
Knocknamuck South	113 0 36	Waterford .	Coshmore&Coshbride	Lismore and Mocollop	Lismore .
Knocknamuck Upper	146 1 12	Wicklow . .	Upper Talbotstown .	Ballynure . .	Baltinglass .
Knocknamucky .	217 2 12	Clare . .	Bunratty Upper .	Inchicronan .	Tulla .
Knocknamullagh .	335 1 7	Cork, E.R.	Cork . . .	Carrigaline . .	Cork .
Knocknamullagh or Derryilan .	212 1 18	Monaghan .	Farney . .	Donaghmoyne	Carrickmacross .
Knocknamunnion .	314 1 19	Wicklow . .	Upper Talbotstown .	Donaghmore . .	Baltinglass .

A portion of a page from the townland "Bible." In order for it to be read, the outer columns have been cropped; they contained the Ordnance Survey Map reference numbers and the 1851 census co-ordinates.

Baronies

Baronies were ancient land divisions that sometimes overlapped counties. Most of the time, you can do your research without paying attention to them; however, some church records, poor law unions, electoral districts, and land records were arranged by barony. I have even seen someone list their barony as their birthplace on a document.

The Householder's Index, which listed the occurrences of surnames in the tithe applotments and the Griffith Valuation, was arranged by county, barony, parish, and townland. Now with computerized indexing of those collections, the *Householder's Index* has become redundant for genealogical research.

Poor Law Unions

Besides administering social welfare programs, the poor law unions also managed civil registrations over a wide area that might cover several counties. You might find some civil registrations of marriages (after 1845 for Protestants and after 1864 for Catholics), and births and deaths after 1864 for people in Inishmacsaint Parish in County Fermanagh being recorded at Ballyshannon in County Donegal, because the Ballyshannon Poor Law Union covered their portion of County Fermanagh. Similarly, your people's vital events might be registered outside of their county.

Electoral Districts

Census taking and even poor law union records were linked to district electoral divisions (DED). The electoral districts were sections of individual poor law unions.

Again, most genealogical research can ignore the electoral divisions, because of the computerized 1901 and 1911 census databases. If you are actually using the census microfilms you will have to search according to electoral district.

In the poor law union registers, you will find the townland and the electoral district given for the people, but not the parish. If there is more than one townland of the same name in the county, you will need to determine the proper parish for your person. You can consult a list of townlands for each electoral district. One such list has been published by George B. Handran: *Townlands in Poor Law Unions*. It provides the electoral districts, the parishes within them, and the townlands of those parishes.

Probate Districts

Another division that you may encounter in your research has to do with probate regions for the processing of wills. These probate regions can cover several counties. Brian Mitchell's *A New Genealogical Atlas of Ireland* (second edition) shows the probate districts.

CHURCH REGISTERS

Now that you have identified the parish and even the townland of your ancestor, you can begin to determine what church registers might be available for that location. Most church registers start around the 1790s, but I have examined some from the middle of the 1600s.

Usually, people were baptized in the Church of Ireland, because it was the state church, but you might also find them in Methodist, Presbyterian, or Catholic records. Do not presume that a person's religion in North America or elsewhere was the same as it had been in Ireland.

Irish marriages usually took place in the home parish of the bride, so if the groom was from another parish, it is wise to consult the churches of neighbouring parishes to find information on him and his family. People usually found their mates within a ten-mile radius of their home, unless they were in the military, the police, or the professions. Burials could take place almost anywhere, but were usually in the churchyard closest to where the deceased had lived or where they had a past association. At times, ministers for other parishes might serve as *locums* when a local minister was sick or away, and they may have recorded the information in their own registers. This might also happen when ministers served multi-point pastoral charges.

I know of one Church of Ireland minister whose pastoral charge extended over four parishes, three counties, two countries, and three dioceses. It is possible that marriages performed by him could be found in the parish registers of any of the churches that he served, if the couple came to where he was ministering at the time.

Because the Church of Ireland and the Methodist Church were closely connected, you might find records of baptisms, marriages, and burials performed by the Church of Ireland ministers copied into the Methodist registers.

PRONI in Belfast has an excellent list of all the church records it has in its collection, including some churches outside of the current borders of Ulster. It also refers to records in local custody. This list can be examined on PRONI's website, so you can plan your research trip accordingly. The site *www.progenealogists.com* lists the holdings of the Church of Ireland's archives, the Representative Church Body Library in Dublin. Its records are mostly for the Republic.

James Ryan's *Irish Records: Sources for Family and Local History* catalogues church records by county and denomination for all of Ireland, but it is somewhat out of date. John Grenham's *Tracing Your Irish Ancestors* (third edition) has, by county, included the microfilm numbers for Catholic registers that are held in the National Library in Dublin.

ONLINE LAND RECORDS

Ever since the tithe applotments indexes and the actual *Griffith's Valuation* images have been put online, you can also narrow down your research within the counties, providing that your ancestor was enumerated in those records. Remember that they only supply the name of head of the household, but this may help you to locate your family within the time frames that these collections cover. Positive identifications of people can only be made when the land records, the parish registers, and civil registration entries match.

FREEHOLDERS LIST

Another way to narrow down your research to the parish and townland is to check the additional computerized records that are held by PRONI. It has digitized lists of people in Ulster from the mid-eighteenth century who were eligible to vote; their townlands are given.

ULSTER COVENANT, 1912

In 1912, when home rule was being discussed for Ireland, British loyalists and the Orange Lodge circulated petitions calling for people to remain loyal to Great Britain. Almost half a million men and women responded to the petitions. The men signed the Ulster Covenant; women signed a special declaration form affirming their loyalty. PRONI has digitized the original documents that contain the signatures and the townland of those who signed. You may find your ancestors or relatives in the free digitized images on the PRONI website.

A page from the Ulster Covenant, 1912. Names and addresses are listed.

RESEARCH REVIEW

If searching the land records has not yielded sufficient clues to the parish of your Irish ancestors, it is wise to review all of your past research results to see if you have missed anything. Re-examine military attestation records, military births and marriages, passenger lists, online parish registers, and cemetery indexes that are available for that county. Similarly, check pre-1901 census fragments, and civil registrations for people of that surname within the county. There may be family members who stayed on the townland. You can check the 1901 and 1911 census, available through the National Archives of Ireland site, to see where people of your surname were living at the time.

If you have identified the county and parish of your ancestors, you are now ready to visit the archives and records offices in Ireland. Even if you have not been able identify the parish before you go, you might yet find your people in the church registers of the county, or other documents housed in the various Irish archives. Not everything has been put online. May the luck of the Irish go with you!

CHAPTER FOUR

Strategies for Travel to and Within Ireland

Just as you have done your prior research to locate the counties, parishes, and townlands of your Irish ancestors, it is important to be aware of the conditions that you will encounter while visiting Ireland. You will experience a certain degree of culture shock as you adjust to driving conditions, multilingual signage, and currency arrangements. Forewarned is forearmed.

Language

Gaelic is the official language of the Republic of Ireland, but English is the language of commerce. However, there are places in County Kerry where you might not be answered in English. Northern Ireland, as part of Great Britain, naturally uses English.

Passports

Ireland welcomes visitors from around the world. In most cases, all you need is a valid passport issued by your own country and you are allowed to stay up to three months. European Union members can remain as long as they want. There is a provision, however, that must be noted for non-EU citizens: your passport must be valid beyond six months from the end of your intended stay.

While the Republic of Ireland and Northern Ireland are functionally two separate countries, for practical purposes there is a unified passport control. Arrival at Dublin or Belfast automatically allows you to enter the other division of Ireland. There are no longer any border checkpoints between the two countries.

Air Travel

When booking a flight to Ireland for genealogical purposes, see if you can obtain an upgraded ticket that will allow you a higher baggage weight limit, because you will be bringing back books, reams of photocopies, maps, and souvenirs. The upgraded ticket may also have more perks, such as priority check-in, pre-seat selection, upgraded meals, and so on.

International flights to Ireland arrive at Dublin, Shannon, Cork, Knock, and Belfast, while most planes from North America arrive in Dublin, Shannon, or Belfast. If you have taken an overnight flight, it might be a good idea to catch up on your rest and adjust to jet lag before you begin your research. There are a number of international hotels near the Dublin airport.

LOCAL TRANSPORTATION

There is an inexpensive ground transportation system of buses and coaches from the airports to the city centres. Some hotels offer free shuttle service to their locations. Avoid taxis, if possible, because they are very expensive.

If your research is confined to Dublin or Belfast you do not need to rent a car. Driving in Dublin is a headache and finding parking is always a problem. In the cities, the names of the streets can change every block, making things more confusing. Also, signage for the side streets can be mounted on walls or the sides of buildings.

Walking

Most of the genealogical resource centres in Dublin are within walking distance of one another. There are also walking tours of historical sites within Dublin. In terms of Belfast, most resources are also centrally located, either within walking distance or a bus ride.

Buses

The local bus systems can take you where you want to go. It might be wise to obtain a Rambler pass for Dublin, which allows you unlimited bus travel for a set number of days. Metro Smartlink cards also exist for Belfast's transit system. Such passes are available at the information offices and many stores. Special literary or heritage bus tours are available around Dublin and Belfast.

DART

A rail system called DART operates between Dublin and its southern and northern suburbs of Greystones and Howth. It was the world's first urban railway system, established in 1834. Tickets can be purchased with credit cards from the dispensers at the stations. Some of those suburban stations have good parking lots. Pearce Station is centrally located, near Trinity College and the south side of the downtown core of Dublin.

LUAS

Within Dublin there are two rapid light rail systems called LUAS. One line operates east and west on the north side of the River Liffey and then goes to the southwest portion of the city. Another line goes south from St. Stephen's Green, close to the National Library and the National Archives. For schedules visit *www.luas.ie*.

Getting Around Ireland

A passenger railway system runs north and south between Wexford and Belfast. Additional lines go to Waterford, Cork, Limerick, and Galway. If you desire to get out to the rural regions, bus transportation will take you to most towns throughout Ireland.

To get out to the parish churches, you may need to rent a car. You will not want to pay for a taxi idling while you search cemeteries for that elusive ancestor. Car rental, however, should be arranged in the larger cities.

CAR RENTAL

Most international car rental agencies, such as Hertz, Budget, Avis, etc., operate in Ireland, along with local rental companies. My travel agent has been able to arrange car rental or leases through AutoEurope at a third of what I had paid when I arranged it myself. North American driver's licenses are usually honoured.

The largest cost of car rental is the various insurances that can be applied to the rental. If you rent your car with a Visa Gold card, you may be able to decline the damage waiver charges. Ask your credit card company what it covers in the way of insurance for car rentals and get it in writing. Some companies in Dublin add a surcharge if you take the vehicle into Northern Ireland, and picking the car up at the airport may also involve a surcharge.

Read your rental policy carefully. Some companies want you to return the car with the fuel tank full. Others charge you for a full tank upfront, and you can return the vehicle near empty.

It is wise to rent the largest car that you can, as many rental vehicles have limited trunk space. Even if you know how to drive a standard, it is also wise to rent an automatic for your first trip, because of all other factors you will experience while driving in Ireland.

Inspect the vehicle for prior damage and scratches and note these on the rental form so that you will not be responsible for them. Also check out the various controls for light, windshield washers, etc. before you drive off, because they may be different from what you are used to.

THE JOYS OF DRIVING IN IRELAND

If you have not had prior experience of driving in Britain, Australia, or one of the Caribbean islands, driving in Ireland will be one of your biggest stressors. In Ireland they drive on the left; the steering wheel is on the right, and the stick shift is on the left. You usually exit the freeways on the left, and you pass on the right. If you are in any way dyslexic, your blood pressure is apt to spike as you encounter so many different stimuli. Watching a video on YouTube about driving in Britain or Ireland may help acclimatize you beforehand.

In the Republic of Ireland, road signage is in Gaelic (Irish), English, and sometimes German, because of the number of German tourists. The police are called Garda. Call 999 for emergencies. In Northern Ireland, the signage is in English.

Many intersections on the highways and in towns and cities employ traffic circles or roundabouts. You must watch the advanced signage to understand where you are to exit, again on the left. Usually the first vehicle into the roundabout has the right of way, but it is important to be in the proper lane. Yield to vehicles to your right. Do not be afraid to go around the traffic circle until you figure out your exit.

The "M" series highways are similar to North American divided freeways, and are called dual carriageways. Some of them are toll highways — payment is in euros, the common currency of the European Union. "M" and "N" series roads radiate out from the M50, a ring road that bypasses Dublin.

Complicated roundabout signage.

The M50 is also a toll road between the N3 and N4 junctions, but it does not have tollbooths. Cameras take a picture of your license plate and you are responsible for paying the toll by 8 p.m. the next day. The M50 e-flow toll payments can be made at most service stations. If you fail to pay the toll, the car rental agency will charge you an additional fee.

The Republic of Ireland uses the metric system of measurement: distances and speed are in kilometres. If you enter Northern Ireland, you will notice that it uses the imperial measurement system, with distances and speed in miles.

In Northern Ireland, there are several "M" series freeways, but they are not toll roads. The "A" series roads are equivalent to the "N" series in the south. The "B" series roads are equal to the "R" series of the Republic. The police belong to the Police Service of Northern Ireland.

If your car is rented from Dublin, it may or may not have both systems on the speedometer. By multiplying a metric measurement by 0.6 you can get the equivalent speed in the imperial system. For example:

30 kph = 18 mph
50 kph = 30 mph
80 kph = 48 mph
100 kph = 60 mph
120 kph = 72 mph

In the countryside, all of the "R" and "B" roads and country lanes are paved, but they are winding and narrow, with the roadway bordered by hedges or rock walls. There are few shoulders to the roads. When meeting oncoming vehicles, it may be necessary to yield and find a wider spot to pull over to allow them to pass. Sometimes the pavement drops off into a ditch, which could break an axle if you hit it at high speed.

DRE photo 2004.

Trimming the hedges on narrow roads, County Kerry.

Those who are unfamiliar with driving on the left side of the road are apt to hug the far left, hitting the curb or scratching the side of the car on the hedges or rock walls. Also, side mirrors of parked cars can be a hazard. Been there, done that!

You will discover that the posted speeds are often higher than what we would expect for similar situations in our home country. Don't be surprised if you find sheep and cattle wandering the back roads. *Drive carefully!*

As you drive the back roads of Ireland, you will often pass through the middle of farms, with barns and sheds on either side of the roadway. You may wonder if you are trespassing on someone's private property. If the road is paved, don't worry: you are on public property. Unless a road is posted as private property, you are permitted to travel on it.

In the towns and cities, you will notice that the traffic lights are green, orange, and red. But instead of red turning to green, it goes red, orange, then green. Vehicles usually begin to move on the orange signal.

Parking is always a problem in Ireland. Most of the towns and cities were created long before automobiles were thought of. You will find that cars are parked halfway over the sidewalks and often against the flow of traffic. In towns you will find vehicles parked on both sides of the street, with only enough for one vehicle to go down the middle of the road. Because of congestion, some of the towns and cities have one-way streets.

Many towns have a parking system in force. It may be called Pay & Display or Disk Parking. You have to purchase a ticket from the dispenser and leave it on the dashboard. Parking police are quite diligent in enforcing parking regulations. Some places use "clamping," so you cannot ignore the parking tickets.

As you travel the back roads, you will find very little signage to indicate what road you are on. In the Republic they have started

DRE photo 2004.

Narrow streets and unconventional parking are common in Ireland.

putting numbered signs (e.g., L5010) for the back roads, but so far they are not linked to the maps. It is wise to have a good Ordnance Survey map if you are looking for a townland, old church, or cemetery. *An Official Road Atlas for Ireland*, published jointly by the Ordnance Survey of Ireland and the Ordnance Survey of Northern Ireland, has a good set of county maps and of the larger towns and cities. Study the examples of road signage and traffic rules that are included at the front, to familiarize yourself with the conditions. There are also special atlases for Dublin and Belfast.

If you are trying to locate townlands, Philips produces several county atlases for Ulster that show all of the back roads. Discovery Maps can also be helpful, but they do not show all of the townlands.

ACCOMMODATIONS

If money is not an object for you, there is a wide range of fine hotels throughout Ireland; however, you are not likely to experience the real Ireland of your ancestors if you stay in them. There are many other options available, particularly if you are working on a budget.

Bed and Breakfasts

B and Bs are very common throughout Ireland, and various websites offer listings of them. Some agencies can book you into a series of B and Bs, so you make your way around the country with accommodation assured. Self-catering cottages can be found in many locations.

During the summer months, university dormitories in Dublin and Belfast offer an inexpensive means of accommodation. Some of the dormitories have small kitchens where you can prepare your meals from food you have purchased in local shops.

The student residences at Trinity College Dublin are available. They are very close to the archival collections and downtown Dublin. See *www.tcd.ie/accomodation/visitors/*.

The cluster residences at University College Dublin (UCD) in the south part of the city are also a bargain. There is good parking if you have brought a car. From a bus stop, within sight of the residences, you can catch buses going to various parts of the city. The buses can take you downtown, with a stop at St. Stephen's Green, within several blocks of the National Library and the National Archives.

The cluster residences at UCD have self-catering kitchens, and the Centra Store onsite carries a range of groceries and confectionaries. Because these residences are in heavy demand it is important to book ahead long in advance, which you can do at *www.summeratucd.ie/accomodation.aspx*.

Some genealogists stay at Buswells Hotel at the corner of Kildare Street and Molseworth. It is conveniently across the street from the National Library. Visit *www.buswells.ie*.

DRE photo 2008.

University College Dublin student residences. An economical place to stay while researching in Dublin.

The Avalon Hostel is located near the National Archives in Dublin. It has storage lockers for your stuff and a safety deposit box for your valuables, including laptops. See *www.avalon-house.ie.*

Ireland is also an excellent country for camping: *www.camping-ireland.ie* is a website for ninety-four member campgrounds in the Republic and Northern Ireland. A published version of the directory is also available at information centres. There are other directories for additional campsites in Northern Ireland that are not included in the above directory. Many have camping kitchens where you can prepare your meals and eat indoors.

Air Transat, flying out of Toronto, allows you to take camping gear or sports equipment free of charge. Check other airlines to see what their policy is on this.

DRE photo 2011.

Roundwood Caravan Park and Campground, County Wicklow.

Because of the weather and winds in Ireland, it would be wise to bring an all-season tent. Roots Canada and Coleman make a number of tents that work well in Ireland, because the flies reach the ground and they have a special internal coating that keeps in the heat.

We have camped in most counties of Ireland and found that it is a good way to meet local Irish and international visitors. If you are camping, it is almost essential that you have a rental car to get from the campsite to the areas of your research. There are no camping grounds within Dublin, but there are some outside of the city, and it is possible to commute in from Roundwood, Carmac Valley, or Rush via DART or the bus system. In suburban Belfast, there is a campground in Dundonald.

Another option is to rent a motor home that you can take to camping and to caravan (trailer) parks. This would provide you with greater comfort than tenting and would also provide you with transportation. Finding sufficient parking for the unwieldy motor home near research centres might be a problem, though.

Shopping

Tesco and Dunnes are major department stores that sell food. Asda, a subsidiary of Walmart, can be found in the some of the towns and cities of the north. Spar and Centra are common grocery stores available in most towns.

Meals

In Ireland you can find many familiar fast food outlets: KFC, Burger King, McDonalds, and Subway. Even Tim Hortons is present, but its coffee and donuts are sold in some service stations or Spar or Centra stores.

Most service stations and grocery stores serve hot food at noon for takeout (or take away). Some do have tables where you can sit down and eat. Many pubs also offer good food. Be prepared

Tim Hortons in a Spar Store, O'Connell Street, Dublin. Expensive donuts and coffee!

to get several selections of potatoes with a meal: mashed, fries, and potato salad. The cost of supper meals in some restaurants depends on the time that you leave the restaurant. The later the meal, the higher the bill.

You will discover that the cost of meals, whether at fast food chains or fine restaurants, is much higher than you would expect to pay in North America. A deluxe hamburger in a restaurant could cost you $25.00 U.S. or Canadian.

Electricity

Throughout Ireland you will find the 220/240 volt system used for domestic electricity, and it has a three-prong plug similar to what we might see on a clothes dryer or a kitchen range. In North America, we use the 110/120 system. Because of the danger when using the higher voltage, power receptacles have individual switches for each plug-in. Turn off the switch at the receptacle before plugging in or removing an appliance cord. If you don't, touching the prongs could give new meaning to the expression "cultural shock" and you could be electrocuted. You will also notice that most bathrooms have non-conductive strings hanging from the ceilings to operate the lights in those damp areas.

Some larger Irish hotels offer North American voltage and power receptacles, so you can use your laptops, razors, hair dryers, and other appliances that you might bring with you. However, for most places you will need to have a converter to change the power from 220/240 to 110/120 volts. You will also need an adaptor to allow you to plug your two- or three-prong North American cords into the convertor. The convertors and adaptors are often available from Staples Business Depot, Canadian Tire, or Walmart back home. Be sure that the convertor and the adaptor interface.

Another option would be to obtain a small electrical convertor that you can plug into the twelve-volt car lighter receptacle in

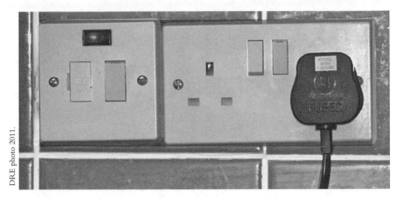

DRE photo 2011.

The 220-volt electrical system in Ireland. For safety, each receptacle has its own on/off switch.

order to charge up your laptop, cellphone, or camera, or to use your razor or hair dryer. These are also available in your home country.

Plumbing

You may also find that the flushing handle for toilets is on the right side and the hot- and cold-water taps are reversed.

Cellphones

Most North American cellphones will not operate in Ireland, unless they are unlocked and a special SIM card is installed. The Republic and Northern Ireland use different cellphone systems. It might be wise to purchase a local cellphone plan for whichever part of Ireland you will be working in. A world phone could solve this problem, but the roaming charges could be very costly.

Internet

Ireland is one of the most "wired" of the European countries, with Wi-Fi readily available. Internet cafés are common, and most public libraries offer Internet service, sometimes for a fee.

CURRENCY

The two Irelands use different currencies. The Republic of Ireland uses the euro, €. It has coinage in 1, 2, 5, 20, 50 cents and 1 and 2 € coins. Its paper currency is in 5, 10, 20, 50, 100, 200, and 500 € units.

Northern Ireland, as part of Great Britain, uses the British pound (£) sterling. Its coins are in 1, 2, 5, 10, 20, 50 pence and 1 and 2 £ coins bearing the image of Queen Elizabeth II. Its bills are in 5, 10, 20, 50, and 100 £ units. There is a range of valid British currencies: Bank of England, Ulster Bank, Bank of Northern Ireland, and Bank of Ireland pound notes. In some of the border counties, both monetary systems are accepted.

Both currencies are more valuable than Canadian or U.S. dollars, and the British £ is more valuable than the European €. Keep this in mind when trying to calculate the relative cost of items in Ireland.

It would be wise to purchase some currency in €s or £s from your home bank before coming to Ireland. If you have to obtain additional currency obtain it from the major Irish banks. Avoid the currency exchanges in airports, because they do not give you the best rates.

Traveller's cheques can be cashed at banks and official Irish currency exchanges. You will find that a surcharge is added to the exchange rate.

Credit Cards and Interac

Finally, a word should be said about credit cards. Visa and MasterCard are commonly accepted throughout Ireland. American Express credit cards are less welcomed. Even if you see credit card symbols in stores or restaurants, check first to see if their credit card system is currently available. I have been caught sometimes when their systems were down and had to use my cash reserves. By using your debit card, you can take funds out of your account back home and avoid the problem of carrying large amounts of cash.

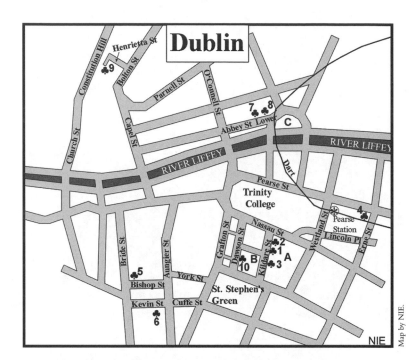

Important places for the genealogist and family historian visiting
Dublin: 1. National Library, 2. National Library Department of
Manuscripts and Heraldry Office, 3. National Museum of Ireland, 4.
Dublin City Library and Archive, 5. National Archives, 6. National
Map Centre, 7. General Registry Office, 8. Valuation Office, 9.
Registry of Deeds, 10. Royal Irish Academy. Other landmarks: A.
Leinster House, B. Buswells Hotel, C. Custom House.

CHAPTER FIVE

Sleuthing the Irish Archival Centres

Family historians or genealogists who visit Ireland will have to go to many archival centres to get access to the documents they need. I have included a variety of them, which range from those catering to amateur family historians to those that seasoned professionals will use to uncover their ancestors' lives in greater detail. I have provided practical information on what to expect at many of these institution and how to use their resources.

THE NATIONAL LIBRARY OF IRELAND, DUBLIN

One of the first places for a genealogist to visit in Dublin is the National Library of Ireland. This grand building is situated on Kildare Street south of Trinity College and is open on weekdays, some evenings, and on Saturday mornings. Check its website at *www.nli.ie/en/homepage.aspx* for hours of operation and holiday closures.

Upon entering the National Library, one passes straight through the rotunda and the security gates. To the left is a locker room where briefcases, coats, purses, cameras, and other items must be stored. You can take a minimal amount of notebooks

DRE photo 2004.

National Library, Dublin, on Kildare St.

into the research areas. Laptops are permitted. After leaving the locker room, to the left are stairs going to a mezzanine floor that has two rooms. The one to the left is the Genealogy Advisory Room, whose staff members will assist you in working with the finding aids it holds, but they will not do your research for you.

DRE photo 2007.

National Library, Dublin. The locker room is through the portal and to the left. The genealogy office is up the first flight of stairs and to the left.

The Genealogy Advisory Room contains a number of important sources: the householders' index for the counties (which has the indexed surnames of the tithe applotments and the *Griffith's Primary Valuation*), an index of the tithe applotment microfilms, many Irish reference works, as well as copies of James Ryan's *Irish Records: Sources for Family and Local History* and John Grenham's *Tracing Your Irish Ancestors*. The latter has a listing of the microfilm numbers for the Roman Catholic parish registers. Ryan's book lists many resources for each county; many of those books and manuscripts are held upstairs in the reading room or the Department of Manuscripts down the street. This room has computer access to *Griffith's Primary Valuation*, the Ordnance Survey maps for the Republic of Ireland, the 1901 and 1911 censuses for Ireland, and other online resources.

After leaving the Genealogy Advisory Room, you will cross the landing to the Microfilm Reading Room, where you will find the Roman Catholic parish registers. If you desire a photocopy of the church record, you will have to take the microfilm back to the Genealogy Reference Room to the microfilm printer there. However, the tithe applotment microfilms and other microfilms can be micro-copied upstairs in a room off the main reading room. Note: When using parish registers or tithe applotment microfilms, here or in other facilities, you may find more than one parish recorded on the reel. In the Catholic parish registers, you may find some of the entries in Latin.

The National Library of Ireland operates a cafeteria on the main floor to the right of the rotunda. If your eyes are burned out after spinning microfilm for hours and you need to give them a rest, you may wish to attend one of the free noon-hour lectures on Irish history or readings from the works of Irish writers, including Yeats, Joyce, Wilde and others. The bookstore also carries a number of important works on Irish history, literature, and genealogy.

For the serious family historian and genealogist, the National Library has many more resources. The reading room upstairs has books, directories, tithe applotment microfilms, and newspapers pertaining to Ireland before and after the partition of 1922. To use them, you must secure a free reader's ticket. You apply for it in a room to the left of the reference counter in the upstairs reading room.

The card catalogue is computerized, and it includes material held in the main library and in the Department of Manuscripts.

You will have to fill in a request form with your reader's ticket number if you want to use its materials. You may have to wait an hour for the materials to be delivered to your desk. There is a photocopying facility for making copies from books.

The Department of Manuscripts of the National Library about a block away is at the corner of Kildare and Leinster Streets. Its entrance is off Kildare Street. The building also houses the Office of the Chief Herald, and you might consult it if you are looking for an ancestor with an aristocratic past.

Access to the Department of Manuscripts requires the reader's ticket, and you can only take a minimal amount of notes or a laptop into the room. Storage lockers are provided on the first floor for your coat, camera, cellphone, briefcase, or purse. The Department of Manuscripts is on the second floor, and you get there by elevator.

Office of the Chief Herald and the National Library Department of Manuscripts, Kildare Street, Dublin.

The Department of Manuscripts contains estate papers — personal and business papers that can often yield important genealogical information. It has photocopying facilities.

NATIONAL MUSEUM OF IRELAND, DUBLIN

After you leave the National Library of Ireland, turn left and you will find Leinster House, the Dáil or House of Representatives, and Senate of the Republic of Ireland. Special tours can be arranged, and in 2008 it was opened up to visits by the general public.

At the west end of the security fence surrounding Leinster House, you will find the National Archaeological Museum of Ireland, whose facade is a mirror image of the National Library. The National Archaeological Museum houses thousands of items that have been found in the bogs: a huge dugout canoe, thousands of gold items, preserved clothing, and pottery and weaponry dating from the Viking period. It will give you an idea of the physical culture of Ireland.

The National Museum of Ireland is free. Photography is not permitted, but its bookstore contains many coffee table books that contain pictures of items in the museum.

The National Museum of Ireland also has another important location, north of the River Liffey, at Collins Barracks, the former military compound on Benburb Street. Besides its other displays dealing with arts, crafts, and technology, Collins Barracks now houses the Irish Civil War (1916–1922) collection that used to be at displayed at the Kildare Street location.

NATIONAL ARCHIVES OF IRELAND, DUBLIN

The National Archives of Ireland (formerly the Public Records Office) is located on Bishop Street several blocks southwest of St. Stephen's Green. To use this facility, you must register at the front desk and acquire a reader's card with a bar code. It is good for a number of years. It will be necessary to use this card to obtain microfilms or to order manuscript collections. To the right is a locker room where you must store your bags, coats, cameras, purses, etc. There is also a dispenser for hot drinks and another for chocolate bars and soft drinks, but food and drink cannot be taken into the reading room.

National Archives, Bishop Street, Dublin. Last building on the right.

A minimal amount of notes are allowed in the reading rooms. You then take the elevator to the fifth floor, where the reading room is located. There is a Genealogy Advisory Service available for those who need assistance with the finding aids. Don't overlook this service, because even seasoned genealogists should always update their knowledge of what the facility contains.

The National Archives has a wealth of genealogical material:

- Tithe applotment films
- Printed *Griffith's Valuation* books
- Some of the microfilmed Church of Ireland parish registers
- Quaker records
- The 1766 religious census
- The 1901 and 1911 Irish censuses
- Pre-1901 census fragments
- The 1908 pension applications that used the 1841 and 1851 censuses in order to establish age
- Prior searches of Church of Ireland baptismal records for the 1908 pension authentication
- Indexes to the marriage bonds
- School records
- Prison records
- Records of those who were transported to Australia
- Union records
- Abstracts of pre-1858 wills
- Health records and other government documents
- Coroner's inquests
- Dáil records, 1919–1924
- Estate records
- Business papers
- Various private collections.

Remember that the National Archives of Ireland contains information for all of Ireland pre-1922 and government documents belonging to the Republic after 1922, as well as some material for the post-1922 north as well.

One of the advantages of doing research at the National Archives is that many of the microfilm readers have micro-printers attached. There is also a large photocopier for flat materials. In planning your research trip to the National Archives of Ireland, consult the website *www.nationalarchives.ie* to review its holdings.

DUBLIN CITY LIBRARY AND ARCHIVE, DUBLIN

The Dublin City Library and Archive at 138-144 Pearse Street is often overlooked by genealogical researchers. The archive upstairs has a fine collection of city directories, microfilms of the civil registration books, civic government records, legal documents, tax rolls, voter's lists, indexes to many church parish registers for Dublin, microfilms of Royal Irish Constabulary service records, cemetery records, peerage books, biographical dictionaries, and much more.

Dublin City Library and Archive, Pearse Street.

For your convenience, there is a restaurant on the first floor. Obtain a library card that gives you access to an Internet terminal to email or do other research.

REPRESENTATIVE CHURCH BODY LIBRARY

The Representative Church Body Library is the archives of the Church of Ireland (Anglican). It holds many of the surviving original Church of Ireland parish registers and vestry minutes for the Republic of Ireland, in addition to materials from various diocesan archives.

This facility is located at Braemor Park in South Dublin on the #14 bus route. Get off at the Mount Carmel Hospital and walk south about two blocks to the RCB Library. You are not permitted to photocopy the parish registers, but you can copy them by hand. Certified extracts are available for a €10 fee. The website of the RCB is at *www.ireland.anglican.org/index.php*. Click on Genealogy.

Representative Church Body Library (Church of Ireland Archives), Braemor Park, Dublin.

Raymond Refausse's *Church of Ireland Records* is a good introduction to Church of Ireland records held at the RCB Library and elsewhere. The RCB Library also has a printout of the parish registers that it holds; it can be purchased for €10.

If you drive there, you will find that the parking lot is small. To get into the building, you have to push the call button and be buzzed in. Lockers are provided for your things; only a minimal amount of notes or a laptop are allowed in the reading room upstairs, and you have to use only pencils for making notes. You will have to register before being allowed to use its resources.

The building is closed between 1:00 and 2:00 p.m. and has no lunchroom. Meals can be obtained in the cafeteria at Mount Carmel Hospital.

GENERAL REGISTER OFFICE (GRO), DUBLIN

The General Register Office for Ireland is located in the Irish Life Centre, north of the River Liffey on Lower Abbey Street. It is housed on the third floor of Block 7. Enter the concourse to the left of the large water fountain and statue and go through the doors to the right, which give you access to the Irish Life Shopping Mall. You will find another set of doors, marked General Register Office, straight ahead. Go through them and register at the desk if a clerk is there. If there is no clerk, take the elevator to the third floor and turn right.

GRO has photocopies of the civil registrations of births and deaths from 1864, Protestant marriages from 1845, and Catholic marriages from 1864 up until December 1921 for all of Ireland, but only from January 1922 onward for the Republic of Ireland. For vital events that happened in Northern Ireland from January 1922 onward, you must obtain the certificates from GRONI in Belfast

DRE photo 2008.

Irish Life Complex, Lower Abbey Street, Dublin. It houses the General Register Office and the Valuation Office.

The research room has the yearly index books. You need to check the quarterly returns for each year after 1878. The research room charges a general fee of €20 per day for complete access to all of the index books. Should you want to search only a five-year period of births, marriages, or deaths, the fee is €2 per five-year set in each of those three categories. After you have done your searches, you will have forms to fill out. Record your name, the name of the person's whose certificate you want, as well as the year, quarter, volume number, and the certificate page number from the index, and hand it to the clerk. The cost of each photocopy is €4. The certificates will be brought out when copied.

A common complaint is that the GRO facility in Dublin is not very genealogy-friendly. It only allows you to obtain five certificates per day. It will mail you copies beyond the five, but that is not helpful, because civil registration research is often a fishing expedition and you need the copies while you are still available to research in Ireland.

DRE photo 2008.

Irish Life Complex. The door to the GRO is through the concourse to the left of the statue and water fountain. The Valuation Office is on the main floor of the building to the right of fountain.

Courtesy of GRO Ireland.

—— (female). 0. Parsonstown		3	588
Collis, Archibald. 0. Naas		2	831
—— Catherine. 100. Ballina		4	12
—— John. 27. Dublin. South		2	628
—— Mary. 54. Limerick		5	348
—— Robert. 0. Naas		2	831
—— Wm. Cooke. 84. Fermoy		4	605
Colloly, Elizabeth. 80. Castlereagh		4	106
Collopy, Honorah. 40. Limerick		10	299
—— Michael. 52. Limerick		5	357
—— Thomas. 60. Kilmallock		15	212
Colloston, Catherine. 35. Mallow		5	466
Collory, Darby. 60. Tralee		5	545
—— Jerry. 0. Tralee		10	468
Collum, James. 1. Lurgan		6	497
—— Margaret. 52. Enniskillen		7	47
—— Peter. 1. Granard		13	115
Collvan, Mary. 24. Cork		5	175
Colly, Anne. 15. Mullingar		3	812

A sample of a page from the civil registration of deaths. You order the certificates by year and quarter, place of registration, volume and page.

Joyce House, the former GRO on Lombard Street, Dublin. You can still obtain certified copies of civil registrations from this office, but it no longer has a research room there. You must get the reference numbers from GRO's Irish Life location.

If you are going to GRO, take along your wife, kids, your mother-in-law, and the dog and cat and have each put in a request for five certificates. If you desire an official copy of the birth, marriage, or death registration, they can be obtained from the old GRO office at Joyce House, 8 Lombard Street East, at a cost of €10.

Another way to avoid the limit of five certificates per day is to go to the GRO headquarters in Roscommon, County Roscommon. The office is located behind the monastery on Convent Road. The GRO office there does not have a public research facility, but if you know the references for the certificates you want after searching the Irish vital civil registrations at the Irish Life Building or through *www.familysearch.org*, the staff can provide you with unlimited number of certificates very quickly. This is the office to which you can also fax your certificate requests. For further information, consult *www.goiroireland.ie*.

REGISTRY OF DEEDS, DUBLIN

One of the important resources for the serious genealogist is the Registry of Deeds at the top end of Henrietta Street, behind the King's Inns on Constitution Hill. The registry holds copies of wills, land sales, land leases, marriage contracts, various indentures, etc., that were registered there from 1709. These documents were copied into large, heavy ledger books the size of medium tombstones, hence the books are often called "tombstone books." There are thousands of these volumes housed in the building.

There are two systems of indexes for these legal instruments: yearly by grantor or by county, parish, and townland. Unfortunately, there is no index for the grantees, but a current

DRE photo 2006.

Registry of Deeds, Constitution Hill, Dublin.

voluntary project is creating an electronic index of all names included in the documents.

To work in the Registry of Deeds, you must register and obtain an electronic card that gives you entry to the various sections of the building. It is valuable to have a staff member give you a tour, because there is a certain learning curve involved. Genealogical researchers will be using three different parts of the building.

If you do not know who the grantor might be, you should search the activity regarding the townland. Go through each year's volume or volumes and see what activity is recorded against the townland in question. You will find the name of the grantor, the grantee, volume number, page number, and instrument number written out by hand. Once you have that information, you then go to the room where the instrument books are kept. They are housed flat in high shelves, and you will need to use a mobile

DRE photo 2008.

Townland Memorial Indexes, Registry of Deeds. You can search them from 1709 by year, county, and townland.

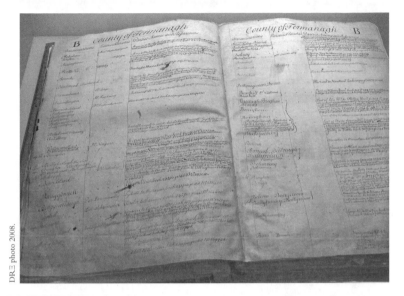

DRE photo 2008.

An example of a page from the Townland Memorial Index. It will give you the grantor, grantee, volume, page, and instrument number. You then take this information to another room where you can view the specific volumes.

staircase, much like you see in Home Depot, in order to get the tombstone books down. The books are often very dusty, and your clothes will get dirty. They weigh between eighteen and twenty-two kilograms (roughly forty and fifty pounds). After taking the books to a reading counter, you can inspect and copy out the information or you can order a photographic reproduction of the pages you desire. Land leases and marriage contracts often contain genealogical information.

If you are tracing the activities of someone who was a grantor, you will need to search the indexes in the room that houses the grantor indexes. Again, the indexes begin in 1709 and list the grantor; the properties in question; and the volume, page, and instrument numbers. You will then go to the room that houses the instrument books.

VALUATION OFFICE, DUBLIN

After you have identified your ancestor's townland and located them in the *Griffith's Primary Valuation*, you may wish to track the subsequent leases and ownership of the property in question. For property that is now part of the Republic, this can be done at the Land Valuation Office at the Irish Life Centre on Lower Abbey Street. This is in the same complex of buildings that house the GRO, where you can obtain the vital records. The Valuation Office is to the right of the water fountain and statue and is on the main floor. For those properties that became part of Northern Ireland, the records are at PRONI in Belfast.

The land valuation books record the post-Griffith's transactions, including changes in leasers and land sales, in coloured ink. There is a fee charged for doing the land searches. Consult the website of the Land Valuation Office: *www.valoff.ie/Research.htm*.

FAMILY HISTORY CENTER, DUBLIN

The Church of Jesus Christ of Latter-Day Saints (Mormons) operates a research facility in Dublin at the corner of Finglas Road across from Glasnevin Cemetery. Disappointingly, it did not have a full complement of the Irish BMD and other microfilms that are available from Salt Lake City.

SOCIETY OF FRIENDS LIBRARY, QUAKER HOUSE, DUBLIN

The Society of Friends (Quakers) operates a library and research facility in south Dublin. The Quakers kept some of the most detailed genealogical records of any religious body in Ireland for their communities and they also often included non-Quakers in their records. The Quakers were also very active in providing relief services during the famine. There is a detailed index for names found in their records that date from the mid-1600s.

Quaker House is located off of Highway R115 (Stocking Lane) south of the M50 ring road. Bus 74A will also get you there. Because its research room has limited hours, see its website for details: *www.quakers-in-ireland.ie.*

METHODIST CHURCH RECORDS, CHRIST CHURCH, SANDYMOUNT, DUBLIN

There are a number of hard-copy Methodist church registers for the Dublin region held at Christ Church, a united Presbyterian/Methodist congregation in Sandymount, a suburb in south Dublin. It is located in the centre of Sandymount village.

TRINITY COLLEGE, DUBLIN

The library of Trinity College in Dublin is known for the famous Books of Kells, but it also holds many resources important to the genealogist. British parliamentary papers and sessional papers contain a vast amount of material dealing with Ireland. It also has digitized Irish and British newspapers.

The Manuscript and Archives Research Library holds more than twenty thousand collections of material pertaining to the history of Ireland and its people. Genealogists can find information in deeds from the twelfth century onwards, the 1641 Rebellion Depositions, the student records of Trinity College, estate papers of the landed families, and material on the 1798 Rebellion and the Easter Uprising of 1916.

Consult Trinity College's website, *www.tcd.ie/Library/manuscripts/collections*, for more information on its library and archival holdings.

ENECLANN

Eneclann is a private company affiliated with Trinity College that conducts historical and genealogical research in Ireland. Its office is in an industrial complex at 1b Trinity Enterprise Centre, Pearce Street. It also produces a variety of Irish research CDs of city directories, tithe defaulters, cemetery inscriptions, and reproductions of historical books. It is one of the partners in Find My Past Ireland. It is not really set up for retail operation, but you can buy its CDs there.

NATIONAL MAP CENTRE, DUBLIN

If you find yourself in need of good geographic sources, the National Map Centre at 1 Church Lane, off of Kevin Street, a block south of the National Archives, is a good place to go. It carries Ordnance Survey maps, Discovery Maps, highway maps, and street atlases.

THE PUBLIC RECORDS OFFICE OF
NORTHERN IRELAND (PRONI), BELFAST

PRONI is the main research facility in Northern Ireland. In 2011 it moved from its former location on Balmoral Avenue to its brand-new facility in the Titanic Quarter, east of the downtown core.

If you are driving there, drive east past Belfast City Hall to the end of Chichester Street to the T-intersection at Victoria Street. Turn left onto Victoria and go north until you see the signs for the Odyssey Complex. Turn right onto Queen's and then right again onto Oxford. Get in the left lane and cross the Queen Elizabeth Bridge, staying in the left lane, and turn left toward the Odyssey Complex. Stay in the left lane again, and just past the Odyssey Complex, before the CitiBank Building,

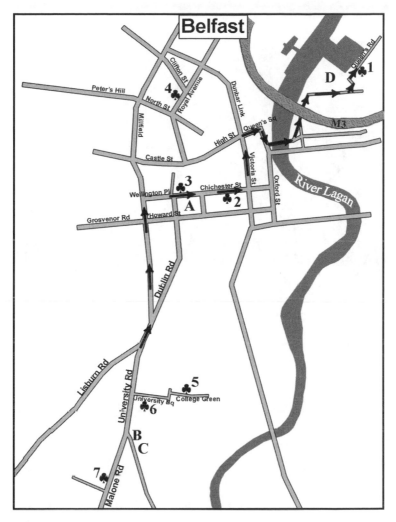

Important landmarks and archival centres for the genealogist visiting Belfast. 1. *PRONI: Public Records Office of Northern Ireland,* 2. *GRONI: General Register Office of Northern Ireland,* 3. *Linen Hall Library,* 4. *Belfast Central Library,* 5. *Presbyterian Historical Society Library,* 6. *Queen's University,* 7. *Ulster Historical Foundation.* A. *Belfast City Hall,* B. *Botanic Gardens,* C. *Ulster Museum,* D. *Odyssey Complex. Arrows indicate route to PRONI through the one-way streets of the downtown core.*

PRONI: The Public Records Office of Northern Ireland, Belfast.

there is a left turn onto Queen's Road. PRONI is next to the CitiBank Building.

If you continue about a quarter mile beyond PRONI, you will see a long three-storeyed red-block building on the left. Immediately to the right of the middle of the building there is a temporary pay parking lot for PRONI. Since this was temporary at the time of writing, it is best to check the PRONI website to see what parking arrangements are in force: *www.proni.gov.uk*.

To use PRONI, you must register at the reception desk, where a photo identification card will be created. For those who have not used PRONI before, staff members will advise you on how to use the facility and what resources will be helpful for your research needs. It has many handouts dealing with genealogical matters.

Lockers are provided for coats, briefcases, purses, and cameras. They are operated by a returnable £ coin. A limited amount of notebooks and files are allowed in the research room. Even more restrictions pertain to the reading room, but laptops are permitted. No pens are allowed in the reading room.

The electronic identification card and its number will allow you to enter the research and reading rooms and order documents and special microfilms from the computers in the research room on the second floor. After you have ordered documents from the computer, you will be assigned a desk, and monitors will indicate when the documents for your desk are ready. You can then pick up the documents from the counter in the reading room.

While PRONI's mandate primarily involves the records of Northern Ireland, including government documents, it does contain material from the historic province of Ulster, some of whose counties remained with the Republic of Ireland since 1922. PRONI has a number of probated wills and land leases pertaining to the former counties of Ulster: Monaghan, Cavan, and Donegal. The church records often overlapped the counties and the border. As well, some of the private papers of the landed gentry contain considerable material from counties in the Republic, because they had wide-ranging land holdings.

The staff of PRONI has created an impressive set of finding aids for their collections. Some of those finding aids then point to more detailed finding aids for individual collections. It is important to master these resources in order to have a productive research experience.

For example, PRONI has church parish registers for most of the religious denominations of Northern Ireland; most are on microfilm and some are originals or hard copies. There is a general finding aid for church records in the research room and also in the microfilm room. It will give you to the pertinent call numbers for microfilms or hard-copy documents for the various church records, such as MIC, CR, D, or T. On the computer system, there are even more detailed MIC indexes for the church microfilms. These will help you identify specifically which reels of film you need to examine. Likewise, there are CR, D, and T finding aids in the computerized catalogue that provide more detailed information about the collections; for example, it will note what hard copies of church records are available and what restrictions might apply to their use. Using the information from the finding aids, these documents can be ordered and brought to the reading room.

The majority of church records are available in the self-service microfilm cabinets in the research room. Most of the Church of Ireland parish registers have been microfilmed twice. The second set is in the MIC583 series. Both sets are often poor in quality and it is wise to consult both versions if available. If possible, it might be necessary to consult the hard copy of the register or a transcript if it is open to the public. It is hoped that a new digitized version of the originals will become available. The church microfilms also often contain vestry minutes that can contain considerable genealogical information, because the vestry looked after both the temporal and spiritual needs of the church and wider community. There are two microfilm printers in the research room. Photocopy cards can be purchased from the document collection counter.

Similar finding aids are available for educational, county records involving health and Board of Guardians documents, including Poor Law Union minutes and registers, estate papers, map collections, Land Valuation Records, business papers, and private collections. Obtaining the correct call numbers from the more detailed guides will save you considerable research time.

In the past, when private collections were being accessioned, there was an attempt to index most surnames found in the documents. These formed a large card catalogue that is now on the computer. Also, in the research room, PRONI has a computer-ized database for many of the post-1858 probated wills. Many of these probates are digitized.

PRONI has digitized the Freeholders' Indexes, 1912 Ulster Covenant, street directories, and some of its finding aids and put them online through the PRONI website, *www.proni.gov.uk*, so you can do preparatory research. Patrons at PRONI also have Internet access to the 1901 and 1911 digitized censuses of Ireland, as well as some other external genealogical databases. Unfortunately, there are no facilities in the research room for printing copies of the 1901 and 1911 census returns from the computers.

The research room also has copies of the printed *Griffith's Primary Valuation* books and city directories, as well as the Bible of Irish genealogy: *The General Alphabetical Index to the Townlands and Towns, Parishes and Baronies of Ireland*. If you desire copies of documents being examined in the research or reading room, you have to fill out an order form and a staff member will arrange for the copying.

The PRONI library also has a number of important books and publications for genealogists, including the *Memorials of the Dead* series, the *Ordnance Survey Memoirs*, and cemetery indexes for parts of Counties Antrim, Down, and Fermanagh.

PRONI has a cafeteria onsite on the main floor. It also has monitors to indicate when your ordered materials are available in the reading room.

LINEN HALL LIBRARY, BELFAST

The Linen Hall Library, across the street from Belfast City Hall, is the oldest library in Belfast. Founded in 1788, it holds a vast collection of Irish literary works and local studies. Access to the building is from the lane to the left of the building. On the fourth level, there is a large genealogy collection that includes

Fountain Street side entrance to the Linen Hall Library. It is just before the red brick building on the right.

Interior of Linen Hall Library, Belfast. Stairs lead to the genealogy floor.

pedigree charts; indexes to births, marriages, and deaths in the *Belfast News Letter*; transcripts of various parish registers; indexes to Presbyterian ministers; peerage indexes; gravestone inscriptions; indexes to military personnel killed during the First World War; and many others. It also has a large Northern Ireland Political Collection that includes books, journals, photographs, and ephemera: pamphlets, handbills, posters, badges, and other items of that nature.

NEWSPAPER LIBRARY, BELFAST

Connected with the Central Library in Belfast is a newspaper library in a separate building that contains most of the major and many of the local Irish newspapers on microfilm. It is located on Library Street to the right of the Central Library. It has microfilm printing facilities.

DRE photo 2011.

Belfast Central Library. The newspaper library is down the lane to the right of the main library building.

ULSTER HISTORICAL FOUNDATION, BELFAST

The Ulster Historical Foundation is a non-profit historical and genealogical agency providing research services and a publishing program. In 2011 it moved into its new facility at 49 Malone Road, Belfast. It possesses a genealogical research library and has a genealogical database of BMDs, cemetery transcriptions, church registers, the Flax Growers Benefit, and much more. These can be utilized on a fee basis or freely if one is a member. The bookstore also sells copies of more than two hundred titles, including the *Ordnance Survey Memoirs*, cemetery transcriptions, and Church of Ireland clergy indexes. Its website is *http://ancestryireland.com*. Membership allows one to access many of the databases, including History from Headstones, and obtain a reduced rate on parish register transcriptions.

NORTH OF IRELAND
FAMILY HISTORY CENTRE, BELFAST

The North of Ireland Family History Society operates branches throughout Northern Ireland. It has a research centre in Belfast at the Mount Masonic Centre at 45 Park Avenue, but its research library is available to members only. It holds considerable Irish and world genealogy resources, including newspapers, parish registers, and cemetery transcriptions. It also has indexes for civil registrations of Northern Ireland births from 1922 to 1971 and deaths from 1956 to 1971. Membership is worth considering. Check out its site at *www.nifhs.org/rescentre.htm*.

THE PRESBYTERIAN HISTORICAL SOCIETY, BELFAST

The Presbyterian Historical Society is currently located at 26 College Green, beside Union Theological College, Belfast.

Presbyterian Historical Society Library, College Green, Belfast.

Consult the society's website for hours of operation: *www.presbyterianhistoryireland.com.*

Its library deals with Presbyterian history throughout all of Ireland. It has parish registers, session minutes and some presbytery minutes, printed minutes of the General Assemblies from 1840, congregational histories, copies of the Presbyterian microfilms held at PRONI, denominational newspapers and magazines, biographical data on Presbyterian ministers, private papers of Presbyterian ministers, some Congregational Church records, and a large collection of books and pamphlets.

WESLEY HISTORICAL SOCIETY, BELFAST

The Wesley Historical Society has its archives at Edgehill Theological College at 90 Lennoxvale, Belfast. It possesses microfilmed and hard copies of various Methodist church registers. The histories of various Methodist groups are described on their website at *www.irishmethodist.org/about/genealogy.php*.

QUAKER MEETING HOUSE, LISBURN

The Society of Friends (Quakers) has a meeting house in Lisburn at Prospect House, 4 Magheralave Road. It holds original Quaker records dating back to 1675, although microfilmed copies of them are also held at PRONI.

FLAX MUSEUM, LISBURN

In the centre of Lisburn is a free museum devoted to the flax industry and the production of linen. It is well worth a visit, because flax and linen production occupied the lives of so many of our Irish ancestors.

LDS FAMILY HISTORY CENTRE, BELFAST

The Church of Jesus Christ of Latter-Day Saints (Mormons) operates a family history centre at 403 Hollywood Road, County Down, on the east side of Belfast. Its hours of operation are listed at its international *website www.familysearch.org*. It has an incomplete set of indexes and certificates for all of Ireland prior to 1922.

GENERAL REGISTER OFFICE OF
NORTHERN IRELAND (GRONI), BELFAST

The General Register Office of Northern Ireland in Belfast issues copies of the civil registrations of BMDs for Northern Ireland, pre and post 1922. It is located in Oxford House, 49-55 Chichester Street, several blocks east of Belfast City Hall. Its website is *www.groni.gov.uk*.

DRE photo 2007.

GRONI: the General Register Office of Northern Ireland, Oxford House, Chichester Street, Belfast. The entrance to GRONI is by the car and large truck parked on the right.

While genealogists complain about GRO in Dublin, the acronym GRONI is telling. Many consider GRONI a real pain! You usually have to make an appointment in advance to use the research room. It has a limited number of computer terminals that access the BMD indexes. Use of the computerized index costs £14 for each six-hour session.

You must register at the desk to obtain a visitor's pass, and then a staff member will come down and escort you upstairs via the elevator to the research room. He or she will then instruct you on how to use the system, which is very different from

GRO in Dublin. You cannot use the certificate reference numbers that you may have found on *www.familysearch.org* or in the index volumes.

All of GRONI's records for Northern Ireland have been computerized. You must search by first and last name only; putting in second names will not work. You can also search for children's births by using the parents' names. The marriage indexes will show you the names of the spouses, so it is not as much of a fishing expedition.

Once you have a found a possible entry, record the names and reference number on a form you will be given, and the staff member will let you see the image of the document. Your computer fee allows you two free peeks at documents. Additional peeks at documents (verifications) cost £4 each. If you desire copies of the certificates that have been verified, they cost £8 each. They have to be picked up three days later, or they will be mailed to you. If you require a priority copy, they are £18 each and will be produced within an hour.

After you are finished in the research room, you are then escorted back down to the main office to turn in your visitor's pass.

If you need certificates for vital events that were registered in Northern Ireland prior to the end of 1921, it would be advisable to do your research at GRO in Dublin or order them from Roscommon. They are also much cheaper!

QUEEN'S UNIVERSITY, BELFAST

The McClay Library at Queen's University, in its special collections, has a large selection of Irish historical journals that often contain cemetery transcriptions and other matters related to genealogy. The library also has a large collection of Irish and British newspapers, some of which are digitized. For its holdings and hours of operation, consult *www.qub.ac.uk*.

ULSTER MUSEUM, BELFAST

After leaving Queen's University, it is worthwhile to visit the Ulster Museum nearby. In 2010 the museum was awarded the prestigious U.K. Art Fund Prize after a major refitting of the building and its exhibits. Besides materials on Irish natural science, arts, and crafts, there is a special section dealing with the history of "the Troubles."

COUNTY ARCHIVES

Counties in the Republic of Ireland are required by law to operate county archives. (The counties of Northern Ireland do not have their own archives, but much of the historical material has been placed in PRONI.) Do not overlook the county archives. They often possess local documents that have not been sent to the National Archives, such as Board of Guardian minutes, poor law union registers, grand jury and petty session court records, wills and probates, leases, and private papers. The Cork City and County Archives website, *www.corkarchives.ie/genealogy*, contains a comprehensive listing of what it holds. Google the other county archives to find out about their holdings.

LOCAL PUBLIC LIBRARIES

Public libraries in the smaller cities and towns of Ireland often have a local history section that has books of local interest, older bound newspapers or microfilmed copies, cemetery inscriptions, Board of Guardians minutes, and poor law union relief ledgers. The local librarians can be an important resource for identifying people and places; I found that the staff and resources at the Enniskillen Public Library are particularly helpful. The librarians may be able to put you in touch with local historians who have even more specialized knowledge of the area.

TOWN HALLS

Town halls often have copies of the civil registrations for their area, and sometimes they have cemetery transcriptions and burial records. Some even have this information in a computer database.

LOCAL CHURCHES

Not all of the church records have been placed in the major archives; many original or current parish registers and vestry minutes are still held by the churches. Some churches have even published their cemetery transcriptions online. Usually, the clergy will allow you to inspect the older parish registers at their convenience. Remember that the clergy's main responsibility is to provide pastoral care, run meetings, and prepare sermons, not to do genealogy for visitors. Donations to the church poor fund are often appreciated for the time that the minister has to take out of his or her busy schedule to facilitate your genealogical quest. Take along a digital camera or a hand scanner to obtain copies of the documents. Handle the originals with care and never remove pages from the records! You might want to purchase a pair of cotton gloves to take with you for handling documents and other precious artifacts.

ULSTER FOLK AND TRANSPORTATION MUSEUM, HOLLYWOOD

While the Ulster Folk and Transportation Museum at Cultra, Hollywood, northeast of Belfast, does not specifically deal with genealogy, its exhibits are a must if you desire an understanding of how your Irish ancestors lived. The folk museum has re-created a village and rural community by dismantling and moving old buildings from various parts of Northern Ireland to the Cultra Estate. Attendants in period costume staff the folk park. The buildings include humble cottier's huts, various cottage industries for producing turf-cutting spades and weaving, public buildings such as schools and churches, and a variety of village shops with living quarters in back or above. Visiting the folk park can occupy an entire day. There is a restaurant in Cultra House.

Across Highway A2 is the multi-leveled transportation museum that documents Irish transportation from the Stone Age to the present. Its lower levels have railway engines and rolling stock. There is a special section of the museum devoted to the *Titanic*, which was constructed in nearby Belfast. Admission tickets to the folk and transportation museums are available for both facilities or individually. Their hours of operation and special events are listed online: *www.nmni.com/uftm*.

THE ULSTER AMERICAN FOLK PARK, COUNTY TYRONE

The Ulster American Folk Park is located five miles north of Omagh on Highway A5. Like the previously mentioned folk museum, it has re-created rural and urban life in old Ireland by bringing together relocated historical buildings and artifacts. After touring the main museum that features rural and famine conditions, you enter the rural folk park that is spread over forty acres. Its buildings and artifacts illustrate the living conditions of various social classes. You then visit a re-created town and dockyard. After going aboard a famine ship, you exit into "America," where some of the emigrants went. Some of those emigrants, whose houses you have visited in the park, have been documented, and their first homes in the new world have been re-created, from log cabins to finer homes.

This folk park has a restaurant, washrooms, a bookstore, and ample parking. Its website is *www.nmni.com/uafp.*

CENTRE FOR MIGRATION STUDIES, COUNTY TYRONE

On the same property as the Ulster American Folk Park is the Centre for Migration Studies, operated by Queen's University and various Northern Ireland library boards. It has a large library of specialized books on Irish emigration, maps, and a computerized database of ship lists, migrants' correspondence, and other matters pertaining to migration. Its admission is free. Consult *www.qub.ac.uk/cms* for hours of operation and special events.

IRISH NATIONAL HERITAGE PARK, COUNTY WEXFORD

This outdoor museum is located off the N11 highway, three kilometres north of the town of Wexford. It covers the history of Ireland from the Stone Age to the Norman Conquest. The tour starts with an audio-visual presentation in the auditorium and then proceeds out to the thirty-five-acre re-creation of Ireland's past, containing megalithic stone burial sites, Ogham stones, early monasteries, water mills, raths, crannogs, other defensive structures, Viking artifacts, and a Norman castle. Guides are in period costume. For hours of operation and admission fees, see *www.inhp.com/index.html.*

DUNBRODY FAMINE SHIP, NEW ROSS, COUNTY WEXFORD

At New Ross in County Wexford, there is a replica of a famous tall ship that was constructed in Quebec in 1845 and carried timber from Canada, cotton from the southern United States, and

DRE photo 2004.

Dunbrody Famine Ship replica, New Ross, County Wexford. The original of this tall ship, built in Quebec, carried many Irish emigrants to North America during the famine.

guano from Peru to New Ross, Ireland. Famine victims travelled on this "coffin" ship to the new world, including the ancestors of John F. Kennedy. The JFK Trust was responsible for creating this educational facility.

Guides in period costume profoundly re-create the experiences of famine emigrants who travelled in steerage. Aboard the ship is a database of Irish emigrants, which was later published on several *Family Tree Maker* CDs. More about this heritage site can be found at *www.dunbrody.com*.

WICKLOW HISTORIC GAOL, COUNTY WICKLOW

This jail operated for two centuries in the town of Wicklow, housing prisoners whose crimes may have been simply stealing a loaf of bread during the famine, Catholic priests who were arrested for saying Mass while the Penal Laws were in force, or political terrorists from the 1798 Rebellion or IRA activities after 1916. Many people were held there for execution or transportation to North America or Australia. Through the use of live actors in period costume, with the help of manikins, the prison's misery comes alive. For hours of operation of the jail and its admission fees, see *www.wickowhistoricgoal.com.*

In the building, there is the Wicklow Family History Centre, which has a computer database of Roman Catholic and Church of Ireland parish registers for County Wicklow, as well as other genealogical resources for the county. It is a fee-for-service agency.

STROKESTOWN PARK AND FAMINE MUSEUM, COUNTY ROSCOMMON

Another important educational resource for the family historian is the Strokestown Famine Museum on the site of a famine workhouse that operated on a grand estate at Strokestown. The workhouse is now gone, but the museum was created in 1994 in the cathedral-sized stable belonging to the estate. The museum has excellent audio-visuals and you leave with an oppressive and profound sense of the personal impact of the famine on the Irish poor. Separate admission tickets allow you to visit the magnificent Palladian mansion on the property and its special gardens, again illustrating the social disparity between rich and poor. Visit its website at *www.strokestownpark.ie/museum.html.*

DUNFANAGHY WORKHOUSE HERITAGE CENTRE, COUNTY DONEGAL

The Dunfanaghy Workhouse Heritage Centre at Dunfanaghy at the top end of County Donegal is located in the famine workhouse administrative building that was opened there in 1845.

Using documents for one of its inmates, Wee Hannah Herrity, the museum has re-created her life story during the famine. It is worth a visit. See *www.dunfanaghyworkhouse.ie.*

HARBOUR MUSEUM, LONDONDERRY

Besides the interesting walk through and around this walled city, stop into the Harbour Museum on Harbour Square to see its displays on maritime history. In addition, in the same building the Derry City Council operates a fee-for-service genealogy centre directed by noted genealogist Brian Mitchell. They have a database of over one million records. Visit *www.derry.rootsireland.ie.*

SKELLIG ISLANDS, COUNTY KERRY

For the adventurous, the monastic ruin on Skellig Michael off of the southwest tip of County Kerry, pictured on page 14, is worth visiting. Here, monks copied classical works, Bibles, and commentaries prior to the twelfth century while Europe was being ransacked by Vikings and other barbarians.

Boats to the islands leave from Portmagee, depending on the weather. Once you arrive on Skellig Michael, you will have to climb over seven hundred stairs to the bee-hive stone huts on the top of the mountain. It is a strenuous climb. There is also an interpretive centre on Valencia Island that explains the significance of the Skellig Islands.

OFFICE OF PUBLIC WORKS (OPW) HERITAGE CARD

There are many of other historical sites in Ireland that a family historian should visit while doing research in Ireland. Many of them now come under the aegis of the Office of Public Works in the Republic. They include castles, grand homes, prisons, historic

The Office of Public Works Heritage Card will get you into about 100 historical and heritage sites in the Republic of Ireland.

monasteries, archaeological sites, and fine gardens. The OPW Heritage Card, costing 22€, will allow you free access to these sites for a year. Student, senior, and family rates are also available.

There are about one hundred places you can visit using the card, and for some of the larger sites, the normal admission fees for three visits could easily pay for the cost of the card. Among the sites are New Grange, Donegal Castle, Glendalough, Kilkenny Castle, Rock of Cashel, Muckross House, Kilmainham Gaol, Castletown, and Hill of Tara. Visit the website at *www.heritageireland.ie/en* to see how to obtain a heritage card and the list of the places it covers.

NATIONAL TRUST CARD

The OPW Heritage Card does not apply in Northern Ireland. There are, however, a number of fine homes and sites run by the National Trust, such as Florence Court Estate, Coole Castle, Crum Castle, and Mount Stewart House and Gardens. Many of these sites can give one an understanding of how the super-rich landlords lived and the social disparity between the rich and the working poor.

Yearly memberships in the National Trust are costly, but they do give admission and free parking at over three hundred National Trust sites in Northern Ireland, Britain, and Scotland. Individual, family, and pensioner prices are available. Again, the cost of the visiting several of the sites in Northern Ireland could be equal to the annual membership.

CHAPTER SIX

Putting Flesh on Your Irish Ancestral Skeletons

Now that you are working in the Irish archives, you will want to go beyond the vital events in the church registers or the civil registrations of births, marriages, and deaths that you may have found. If you do not find your person in the nearest church records, look at the adjoining parishes or even churches of other denominations for records of vital events.

MARRIAGE BONDS

You may not have found a marriage record for your ancestor in the parish registers, but there is still another way that a partial record of it may have survived. Most people were married after banns were read in the parish church on three consecutive Sundays. Sometimes the information on the banns forms, found in some parish registers, is even more detailed than the marriage registrations.

Often, the wealthy obtained marriage licenses from the bishop so they could hold their wedding in private and immediately. If a groom was not known to the bishop or minister, he would have to post a marriage bond to obtain a marriage license and guarantee that he was legally able to be married. These funds were held for a period time. A marriage license or a marriage bond was not a guarantee that the marriage took place, only that it was intended. In the case of an illegal marriage (bigamy or misrepresentation, for example), there were grounds for annulment and the marriage bond would be forfeited.

The original marriage bond forms were destroyed in the Four Courts Fire, but an extracted list of the marriage bonds was made and has survived. The list, according to diocese, gives the names of the bride and groom and the year. These volumes are at the National Archives. A microfilm copy of the Clogher diocese's list of marriage bonds is available at PRONI and it has been put online at *www.rootsweb.ancestry.com/~nifer/clogher-mar.html*.

Another source of marriage information in the Presbyterian Church registers are applications to a marriage to be held in the church. This was submitted to the Session for approval. They contain information on the bride and groom, their residence, and how long they lived there.

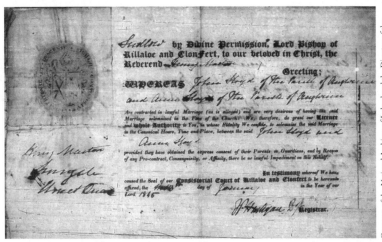

Courtesy of the National Archives of Ireland and the Director of the National Archives of Ireland.

An example of a marriage licence for Aughrim Parish, County Galway, issued in January 1845, NAI MFCI/6.

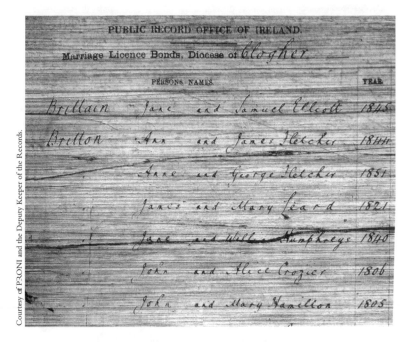

Index to Marriage Bonds, Clogher Diocese.

An example of a Presbyterian notice of marriage for Clogher Parish.

BISHOPS' TRANSCRIPTS

Sometimes, you might find what appears to be a duplicate set of parish registers in the Irish archives. They may be extracts from the original registers, or they may be the periodic reports of baptisms, marriages, and burials that rectors were required to send to their bishops. These bishops' returns, or transcripts, were held at the diocesan offices and were not necessarily sent on to the Public Records Office in Dublin and thus escaped the Four Courts' Fire. Not all of them have survived, however, for other reasons.

It is worthwhile to examine any set of bishops' transcripts you find, because they may not be exactly the same as the regular registers. They may contain more or fewer names than are found in the parish register. Some names were missed and others added at the last minute. In one parish that I am working on, the bishops' transcripts are in better condition than the parish registers, because the parish registers have faded and someone has over-written the entries, making many mistakes in the names, dates, the ages, and the townlands. Be sure to use all the sources that you find, weighing the evidence if you find conflicting information in different versions of the documents.

CONFIRMATION LISTS

Additional sources of information can be found in confirmation lists. Some of the church registers included confirmation lists. They provide the names, townlands, and the ages of those being confirmed.

Church of Ireland confirmation list for 1879, Inishmacsaint Parish, County Fermanagh.

VESTRY MINUTES

Each Church of Ireland had a vestry, who were a group of men from the parish who looked after the physical needs of the church and social welfare needs in the community. Its members could even include Roman Catholics. Most of the vestry minutes have survived, because they were not sent to the Public Records Office at the Four Courts. Within these records, you can find out information about what individuals were doing in their communities.

Vestry minutes might be found in local custody, PRONI, the National Archives, or the Representative Church Body Library in Dublin.

CORONER'S REPORTS

If one of your Irish ancestors died in an accident or under suspicious circumstances there might be a coroner's report that could shed more information on the death, list other family members who were interviewed, and give additional information on the person's life. These may be found in the Republic's county archives, the National Archives of Ireland, or at PRONI.

WILLS AND WILL ABSTRACTS

While all of the pre-1858 wills kept at the Four Courts were destroyed in 1922, there were abstracts made of the wills that might lead you to information on your ancestors. These are on microfilm in the major archives. PRONI has put the post-1858 Ulster wills online. The Quakers also kept copies of many wills.

You may find copies of some of the pre-1858 wills in the papers of various law firms that have been deposited in the archives.

COUNTY BURIAL REGISTERS

Remember that not all family members emigrated; some stayed on the townlands that they had farmed over time. People did not like to give up their ancestral townland, even if they did not own it. You may be able to put the pieces of the genealogical puzzle together by examining their burial records.

Sometime after the beginning of civil registration of deaths in 1864, many counties created burial registers for deaths that occurred within the county, giving names, relationships, townland, age, and the place of burial. These burial registers are often kept in the town hall of the county seat; some have been deposited in the archives. Not all of these burials would have had memorial stones in cemeteries, but it is possible that this burial information might lead you to the parish registers holding information on your ancestral family.

MILITARY MEMORIALS

In similar vein, family members who did not emigrate may have had sons and daughters who later died in the First World War. The Committee of the Irish National War Memorial created memorial books of Irish soldiers. They are available at the National Archives, have been digitized, and can be searched on the Irish section of *www.ancestry.com*. The memorials list name, regimental number, rank and company, type of death, date and place of death, and place of birth.

The Commonwealth War Graves Commission has information on many of the Irish soldiers who died in the First and Second World Wars and where they were buried. The regiment, age, place and date of death, and next of kin are sometimes mentioned in its database. *Visit www.cwgc.org.*

OCCUPATIONAL GUILDS AND PROFESSIONAL ASSOCIATIONS

Not all of our Irish ancestors were tenant farmers; some were tradesmen and belonged to guilds. Others were professional men in the law or the clergy. The alumni records of Trinity College Dublin give the names of the students, their age when they entered, and the names and occupations of their fathers. The Ulster Historical Foundation has published a multi-volume set of biographies of Church of Ireland clergy for most of Ireland. You may find information on guild members at the National Archives or at PRONI.

DIRECTORIES

If your ancestors lived in towns and cities and had a business or a trade, they might be found in various published directories. PRONI has digitized many of the directories for Belfast and the province of Ulster; these are online. The National Library and the Dublin City Archives have a large collection of hard-copy directories for Dublin. A division of Eneclann has put some of the directories on CD.

TOPOGRAPHICAL DICTIONARIES

We should always be trying to find out more information about the context in which your ancestors lived. Samuel Lewis, in the 1830s, conducted an extensive survey of Ireland's towns and cities. He included history and geography on each of the localities, including information on churches, schools, fair days, and local industries. His *Topographical Dictionary of Ireland* is now available on the Internet and on CD.

Included under the subject of topographical dictionaries are the *Ordnance Survey Memoirs*, also done in the 1830s. While the published versions cover current Ulster and part of County Donegal, there is unpublished raw material on some of the counties of the Republic available at the Royal Irish Academy next to Mansion House at Dawson Street in Dublin. Check its site: *www.ria.ie.*

LODGE MEMBERSHIPS

If your ancestor was a member of the Orange Order when he lived in North America or elsewhere, chances are that he had an earlier membership in a lodge when he lived in Ireland. You should check with the Orange Lodges in the county where he lived. There are also some Orange Lodge records in PRONI.

The same thing goes for the Masons. The Masonic Headquarters on Molesworth Street in Dublin has an extensive database of its past members.

POOR LAW UNION RECORDS

The Great Famine had an impact on many of our Irish ancestors, and many may have had to go into the workhouses or take advantage of "outdoor" relief. The ledger books of the poor law unions are filled with information about the people who received assistance: names, ages, occupation, marital status, number of children, and their townland. The workhouse books contain information on the health of the individuals, their religion, and what happened to them, whether they died there or were discharged. Also, the Board of Guardian's minutes may have references to specific individuals. PRONI has a number of poor law union records, while various county archives in the Republic have others. Not all of the PLU records have survived.

LAND RECORDS

If you have found your ancestors in the parish registers, you can now begin to search out more information about the economic aspects of their lives. Once you have their townland names, you can consult the microfilms of the actual tithe applotments to see how much land they farmed or if they had moved to other farms.

Remember that the tithe records listed only the heads of the household and positive identifications are difficult. The enumerations were done over a number of years, so it is wise to check all entries for that townland to see if they increased or diminished their land leases. You can also check the *Griffith's Valuation* to see if the family was living on townland some thirty years after.

ESTATE PAPERS

Because most of our ancestors did not own their own land, they had to lease it from the landlords or middlemen. You can find out the owners' or middlemen's names from the tithes applotments or the *Griffith's Valuation*. Many of the papers of the large landowners have been deposited in PRONI, the National Library, or the National Archives in Dublin.

Among these papers, you may find correspondence involving your ancestors, rent collection books, copies of the parchment leases, and maps of their lease. The leases themselves were usually made out for the lives of three persons (but not necessarily all

Rent book from Archdale Estates, Castle Archdale Museum, County Fermanagh. The left-hand column giving townlands was cropped out in order to reduce the size of the image.

belonging to the same family), giving not only their names, but their ages. The terms of the leases are also important to understand the conditions under which your ancestors leased the land. I have examined a number of these leases dating back to the 1730s.

The land leases were often printed on parchment with blanks left for the names of the leaser, the three lives, and any special rights given and obligations owed to the landlord. Some of the originals can be found at PRONI and the Department of Manuscripts of the National Library in Dublin.

Remember that the large landowners held land in many parts of Ireland. It is important to discover where their papers

PRONI, Ely Papers, D580/237. An example of a lease from 1767 issued by the Earl of Ely to Thomas Brock, Killy More Townland, for additional land on Cornadarum Townland, Inishmacsaint Parish, County Fermanagh. It contains the names and ages of three "lives" and the rights and responsibilities of the leasee.

were deposited. Information on land leased from them in County Kerry might be found in their estate papers in County Antrim or even Britain. Always think outside of the box.

The Registry of Deeds in Dublin has registered leases, land sales, and marriage contracts back to 1709. Similarly, if you are tracking modern land transactions of your ancestors in Northern Ireland post-1921, you may find them at the Land Registry Office, Lincoln Building, 27-45 Great Victoria Street, Belfast. Visit its site at *www.lrni.gov.uk.*

LANDED ESTATE COURT RENTAL RECORDS

After the famine, many of the large landowners were land-rich but cash-poor and had to sell off parts of their holdings. The government stepped in to protect the rights of those who had leased the land. Court surveys were done on the land to be sold, listing the tenants and the conditions of their lease. Some gave the names and relationships of those included in "the lives." The names of the leasees can be searched on *www.findmypast.ie.*

EARLIER FREEHOLDERS LISTS

It is possible to get land lease records of your ancestors back into the eighteenth century. People who owned or leased a certain amount of land were entitled to vote. (Catholics were excluded until 1793.) These freeholders' lists date from 1727 to 1829 and contain information on the freeholder, the address of the person and townland, the landlord, date of registration, etc. Sometimes the "lives" were named. The freeholders of Ulster have been digitized by PRONI and are available on PRONI's website. Copies of freeholder's lists for those counties now in the Republic can be found at the National Archives of Ireland.

REPRODUCTIVE LOANS

In 1824 a microcredit system was established to help the poor set up their own businesses or to improve their circumstances. The National Archives of Britain contains information on many of these loan recipients, including their townland and the status of their loans. The records cover parts of six counties in the Republic and extend past the famine. You can search them on *www.movinghere.org.uk*.

DOCUMENTING IRELAND'S PARLIAMENT, PEOPLE, AND MIGRATION

A recently developed source of information is the new site *www. dippam.ac.uk*. It contains a collection of enhanced British parliamentary papers on Ireland from 1800 to 1922. These digitized official government papers dealing with Ireland, over fifteen thousand of them, often have detailed information, some of which may involve your ancestors.

Another part of that site includes a large database of images relating to emigrant letters, shipping ads, passenger lists, family papers, and other emigration records that have been collected from many of Ulster's record repositories.

A third part of the site includes over ninety interviews with people who had left the original nine counties of Ulster.

OTHER LISTS

You may be able to push back your ancestral history even further by consulting various resources that exist for the counties. Consult Ryan and Grenham's books for them. You might find your ancestor's names in the hearth tax lists, militia muster lists, partial census records, parishioners lists, military land grants, and so on. Some of these have been put online by various archives and genealogical societies.

You will, however, have to be careful in assuming connections between individuals separated by time. With the Irish naming pattern being common, many cousins shared the same forename, and you might be barking up the wrong side of the genealogical tree.

GOVERNMENT COLLECTIONS

PRONI and the National Archives in Dublin have been mandated to collect documents generated by various government departments. Because Ireland was so politically volatile, many people came under the interest of the legal authorities. There are hundreds of ledger volumes in the National Archives dealing with crimes. You may find petitions and legal appeals associated with this. Some of those court records can be found on *www.findmypast.ie*. You may find your ancestors mentioned in those records.

Many British loyalists suffered losses during the 1798 Rebellion. Those who made claims can be searched on *www.findmypast.ie*. It will give you their names, occupations, residences, and the nature of their claims.

PRIVATE COLLECTIONS IN ARCHIVES

PRONI and the National Library's Department of Manuscripts in Dublin have many collections of private papers that deal with politics, companies, employment, and cultural matters. There are good finding aids in both institutions that will help you search out information.

NEWSPAPERS

As with genealogical research done elsewhere, newspapers can be a fountain of information. Do not overlook the newspapers of Ireland. Hardbound or microfilmed copies of newspapers can be found in the local public libraries, the Belfast Newspaper Library, the Linen Hall Library, the National Library of Ireland, Trinity College Dublin, and Queen's University. By immersing yourself in the newspapers for the area you are researching, you will certainly gain an understanding of the conditions under which your ancestors lived, and you may even find actual information about their individual lives.

CHAPTER SEVEN

Digging Around in Irish Graveyards

After you have spent your time in the archives or in local churches looking for your relatives, do not overlook the cemeteries. Headstones may contain information that can make up for lost parish registers. Many times they predate civil registration and can establish relationships between people. They may be the only record that you can find for your ancestor's life in Ireland. Because many Irish headstones have become buried or sunken over time, you might be "digging up your ancestors" as you have to cut away sods covering flat stones.

It is important to check with the church or cemetery owner for permission to undertake serious investigation of the stones if it involves cleaning them or exposing buried ones. In most cases, if the work is done properly, the owners of the cemetery will welcome your efforts.

Remember that because of the cost most Irish people were buried without headstones and also many memorial stones have perished over time. But you may be lucky enough to find a headstone pertaining to your family. On the tombstones you might find information regarding the townlands of your ancestors, migration of family members, and sometimes information on their cause of death.

DRE photo 2006.

St. Molaise Church of Ireland Cemetery, Monea, Devenish Parish, County Fermanagh. Often, flat tombstones can be buried under grass in front of vertical headstones. Changes in grass colour can be indicative of something buried beneath.

Another caveat must be mentioned: although "it is written in stone," the information may not be accurate. Tombstones are sometimes erected years after the event, and the dates and ages might be wrong. People also lied about their ages. You need to check this information against parish registers or civil registrations if available.

You will find a great variety of types of memorials in the cemeteries: simple headstones, elaborate family plots with high Celtic crosses, fenced in burials, sarcophagi, mausoleums, and huge flat or vertical memorial slabs, sometimes with heraldic crests. Some of the larger tombstones can contain information on two, three, and even four generations. They also can contain symbols that refer to lodge associations or occupations.

DRE photo 2011.

Old Kilmurray Roman Catholic Graveyard, County Wicklow. Some gravestones can give you information on occupation and cause of death. Obtaining the death certificate and a coroner's report will give you even more information.

DRE photo 2004.

Grey Abbey, County Down. These tall, vertical tombstones are a goldmine of genealogical information, sometimes listing two, three, or more generations.

Deaths of children are always difficult, emotional times. Their gravestones can often take interesting forms, with euphemistic images of sleep.

St. John's Church of Ireland Cemetery, Fivemiletown, County Tyrone. Child's grave in the shape of a cradle.

Until the disestablishment of the Church of Ireland after 1870, it operated most cemeteries and people of all denominations were buried in them. Depending on the region, you will find Catholic cemeteries that were established in the 1830s after emancipation. Remember that most Church of Ireland cemeteries were once Catholic cemeteries. Many Catholics continued to be buried in them, even though they went to their own churches. On some of the headstones, you will find the text in Gaelic. There are computer programs on the web that can help you translate from Gaelic to English.

As with parish registers and other genealogical documents, you may find differences in the spellings of surnames and townlands

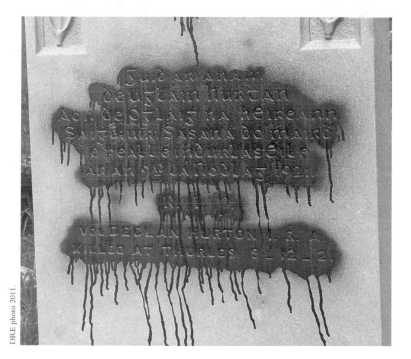

St. Declan's Roman Catholic Cemetery, Ardmore, County Waterford. Vandalized headstone of an IRA member killed in 1921. Text in Gaelic and English.

on tombstones. Do not dismiss those variations as necessarily belonging to a different family. There were no standardized spellings for surnames until quite recently. Many Irish people were illiterate, and their surnames appeared on documents or tombstones as their creators spelled them phonetically. Sometimes you will find various spellings of the surnames as time went on.

Sydare Methodist Cemetery, Magheracross Parish, County Fermanagh. An ideal headstone, giving places of birth, dates, and townlands.

PRECAUTIONS

You need to be prepared before going to research in Irish cemeteries. Some of these graveyards have been abandoned, are isolated, and can be dangerous places. Grass might not have been cut, obscuring hidden stones jutting up from the ground. You could easily stumble over them or slip on the grass or flat memorial stones.

One summer while working in Ireland, I heard of two deaths in cemeteries. A sexton was killed when he slipped and struck his

DRE photo 2008.

Old Magheracross Parish graveyard, County Fermanagh. This grave-yard was very dangerous because the grass was wet and uncut, there were potholes, and also collapsed graves.

DRE photo 2009.

Bangor Abbey, County Down. Tall headstones leaning forward can be very dangerous.

head on the base of a headstone. Another person was killed when a tall headstone fell on top of him — it is easy to fall into potholes and burials that have collapsed. It is best to have someone with you and carry a cellphone for emergencies.

Good hiking boots are essential to protect your feet. Heavy work gloves can protect you from briers that have grown up around headstones. Also, glass can be encountered at the base of headstones as vases have broken over time. You may need to carry pruning sheers to remove briers, a small trowel to remove debris, and a spray bottle of water with soft brushes to clean the stones.

Although Ireland does not have snakes, there are other venomous dangers that can be found in graveyards: fire ants, bees and wasps, and other insects, as well as stinging nettles. Your cemetery kit should include the above-mentioned tools, a field book, insect repellant, first aid supplies, water for drinking as well as for wetting the stones, and a hat to protect your head from sunburn. It does not always rain in Ireland!

One summer it was so hot that my wife Nancy suffered heat stroke while we were working in a cemetery. I thought that she might have to be buried there, perhaps making a good excuse for me to come back to Ireland every year!

Buried stones can often be detected by noticing discolourations in the grass or the growth of patches of moss. Probe the surface with a sharp knife and see if there is something below the surface. Determine the perimeter of the buried object. To get at the buried memorial, cut away the sod. You may even have to cut through tree roots below the surface. Remove the sod and dispose of it in an appropriate place. The minister or the sexton can advise you on what to do with the rubbish.

Some headstones have inscriptions on both sides, while some bases of Celtic crosses or obelisks have inscriptions on all

DRLE photo 2009.

Old Slavin Graveyard, Inishmacsaint Parish, County Fermanagh.
Nancy Elliott cleaning exposed flat tombstones after sods were removed.

four sides. Be sure to check the bottoms of flat or vertical slabs, because important family information may be found there.

PHOTOGRAPHING TOMBSTONES

The best way to record the inscriptions on the memorial stones is to photograph them with a digital camera. Digital photography is a great boon to genealogy, because you don't have to worry about the cost of film. Another advantage of using digital cameras in recording tombstones is that you have a record of the stone that can be examined again and again. The camera can pick up things that you might miss if you only depend on a transcription of the stone that was made on the spot. Also, digital images can be put into the computer and manipulated by enlarging them, reversing them, or enhancing the images to get the most out of them. You can even mend broken stones using Photoshop.

It is best to clean up the memorial stone by removing dirt, lichen, and vines. A soft brush can work wonders in revealing the inscriptions.

Old Slavin Graveyard, Inishmacsaint Parish, County Fermanagh. A soft brush will usually remove lichen, moss, and dirt from tombstones.

Take pictures with the highest shutter speed possible so as to avoid problems of movement. It is best to use a digital camera that allows you to put the viewfinder up to your eye, rather than those that are held at arm's length. Even then, you should stop breathing when you press the shutter release.

Many times it appears that stones have nothing on them, but if you spray some water on them with a mister bottle and brush them with a soft brush, the lettering will become very apparent. On a hot day, allow the surface water to evaporate. The water in

NIE photo 2010.

A digital camera with a viewfinder minimizes camera movement when photographing text on tombstones.

DRE photo 2008.

Garrison Church of Ireland Cemetery, Devenish Parish, County Fermanagh. Using water as a highlighter, different camera angles, and artificial lighting, you can often read stones that would otherwise appear to have nothing on them.

St. Molaise Church of Ireland Cemetery, Monea, Devenish Parish, County Fermanagh. After we turned this curious stone over we found an inscription on the back.

DRE photo 2006.

the indentations will not evaporate as fast and will illuminate the inscription. Taking shots of the inscriptions from various angles can also help to capture the image of the lettering. You can also use the flash or take the picture at a different time of the day, when the sun is shining directly on the stone.

If you are trying to shoot a flat stone and the sun is shining into the camera, move to the position of the sun and shoot the picture in the reverse direction. Try to avoid letting your shadow fall on the surface. You can then put the picture into a photo program and flip the picture around to read the inscription.

Inscriptions cut into white granite are very difficult to photograph. By putting a little mud in your brush and rubbing it over the surface, the inscription will stand out. Be sure to clean the surface after you have taken the picture.

It is important to take multiple pictures of the tombstones, their context, and neighbouring stones, because relatives may be

DRE photo 2007.

St. Molaise Church of Ireland Cemetery, Monea, Devenish Parish, County Fermanagh. After highlighting the inscription with water and putting it into a photo-enhancing program, we were able to decipher the text of the strange stone with the skull and crossbones. Its reads: "Hear [sic] lyeth David R. Anderson, brasser, who died the 5th of Nov. 1685."

buried nearby. Take close-ups of their inscriptions, particularly the numerals, because 3, 5, and 8 can be mistaken for one another, as can 1 and 7 or 2 and 9.

GENEALOGICAL WHEEL OF FORTUNE

Suppose you have a very difficult stone to transcribe. Make a copy of the original photo and always use the copy. Pretend that you are Vanna White and start to identify the individual letters. In some cases, reading a difficult inscription can be made easier by turning the photo into a negative image with an image-editing program. Enlarge it so that you can read the details. Using a paintbrush tool,

St. Molaise Church of Ireland Cemetery, Monea, Devenish Parish, County Fermanagh. This stone dated 1741 was difficult to transcribe.

St. Molaise Church of Ireland Cemetery, Monea, Devenish Parish, County Fermanagh. Same stone as above, taken from a different angle and with the image inverted so that the lettering stands out.

which comes with most photo programs, paint in the letters that you can make out. Use the brush rather than the pencil feature and choose a particular colour for each word. As you continue to identify the letters, the meaning of the inscription should become clear. If you make a mistake, make another copy of your original and start again.

Some inscriptions are almost impossible to read, but there are certain conventions in the wording that can help you decipher the stones: "Erected by … in loving memory of … who departed this life … here lyeth the body of…." You will find creative spelling, wrap-around wording without hyphens, and dyslexic numerals and letters.

St. Molaise Church of Ireland Cemetery, Monea, Devenish Parish, County Fermanagh. Inscription of the stone enhanced with digital paintbrush. Note inverted A's, wrap around lettering, and creative spelling. The stonecutter appears to be trying to convey: "Here lyeth the body of May Eam. She departed this life [in] the 71st [year] of her age, the first [of] March 1741."

179

CHURCH MEMORIALS

Do not overlook the memorial plaques found on the inside walls of churches, the stained-glass windows, and dedication inscriptions on items within the churches. Such inscriptions can contain extensive family information and a social history far beyond what is found on the gravestones.

Church of Ireland Cathedral, Ferns, County Wexford. Memorials on the inside walls of churches can contain more information than is found on tombstones or even in church registers. As in this case they can refer to deaths outside of the country.

HERALDIC CRESTS

On some tombstones, you may find elaborate heraldic crests. Such crests were issued to an individual, and you may be able to get detailed information on his or her family, because the possession and use of crests was dictated by the Chief Herald's

Office. The crests were issued in London, Edinburgh, or Dublin. By submitting a copy of the crest to these offices, you may get surprising information.

Crested monument on a mausoleum, First Broughshane Presbyterian Church, County Antrim. Note the place of residence indicated in the inscription. Legitimate heraldic crests can be a gateway to more information on the family's history.

St. John's Church of Ireland Cemetery, Fivemiletown, County Tyrone. Another example of a crested tombstone, from 1730. Deeply inscribed stones continue to show their text after centuries.

GIVING BACK

When doing research in any cemetery, you should leave it in better condition than you found it. Care must be taken that you do not damage any of the monuments while doing your research. I have heard of people using wire brushes and chemicals on tombstones —you should use nothing more than water and a soft brush. Tweezers or a small knife might be used to remove vines clinging to the inscription.

While there, it would be a tribute to your ancestors to clean up debris around their graves those surrounding them. Fill in potholes where earlier visitors have dug away at the base of sunken headstones, trying to read hidden inscriptions. This will stabilize the headstone and to make sure that someone does not fall into the holes. You may even wish to make a donation to the church's cemetery fund.

INDEXING THE CEMETERY

Another way of giving back is to index the cemetery if it has not been indexed before. While you are researching in the cemetery, you might want to index the whole thing, because there are apt to be other relatives buried there, and you may want to refer back to that cemetery after you have gone home as you discover more relatives. That is how I became involved in cemetery indexing. My earlier archaeological training in Alberta and Italy certainly came in handy. Besides, so much work needs to be done in getting Irish cemeteries indexed, and your contribution will add to the body of knowledge. Also, some of the earlier indexes were poorly done and should be redone now that we have digital photography.

Some people only record their family surname and then post this information on the Internet. This is not very helpful, because family history involves many surnames and the information is not contextualized.

If you are going to index an unindexed cemetery, try to define the cemetery by its natural divisions and then index it row by row within those divisions. Make a simple map showing the location of buildings, roadways, sidewalks, trees, and other features. Because the rows of graves will not be uniform, you will have to make judgment calls on which rows some graves will be recorded in. Mark the rows on your map.

Photograph down the row so you can establish the context of each row. Photograph all of the stones, including the unmarked graves and mounds. In your field book, list the sequence of all stones and spaces in each row. There is nothing worse than trying to find a tombstone using an index that only has an alphabetical list of the surnames without their context.

When you prepare your report on the cemetery, list the tombstones *in situ* (in the sequence that they are found).

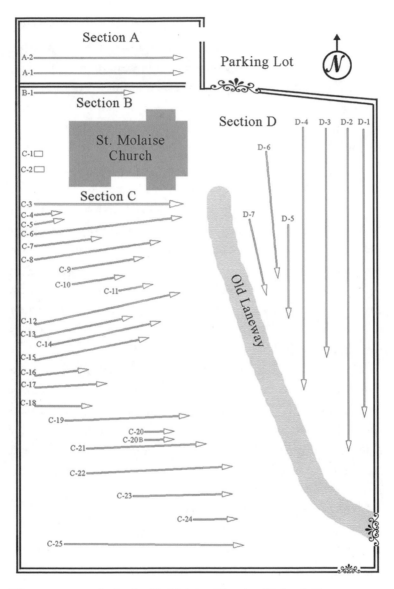

The map we made for the St. Molaise Church of Ireland Cemetery, Monea, Devenish Parish, County Fermanagh, 2007.

Garrison Roman Catholic Cemetery, Inishmacsaint Parish, County Fermanagh. Checking transcription against inscription for accuracy.

Describe each burial type (headstone, flat, Celtic cross, sarcophagus, etc.) and give a full transcription, including the townland names when given.

You may have to decide if you want to include poetry, scripture, or invocations of the saints in your transcription. However, in a common burial ground, the invocation of saints is a good indication that the deceased was a Catholic.

If you cannot decipher some names or dates because of some of the stone has split off (shaling) or other damage, indicate so by using an ellipsis […]. If you have to guess at a date, indicate so by following it with a question mark [?].

At the end of your index, you should include a comprehensive alphabetical index of all names on the tombstones, linked to their locations on the map by section, row, and number in the transcriptions.

Three Old Inishmacsaint Parish Graveyards

Old Slavin Transcriptions

Row 1

1. [spaces].

2. [Raised flat with strange graphics at the top; no dates or other details]. IHS. Erected by **Michael Kelly**.

Row 2

1. [spaces and mounds].

2. [Partially buried flat; inscription has archaic spelling where an "f" was used for "s": *i.e.* Treffey]. Erected by **Patrick Tressey** in memory of his father **Owen Tressey** who departed this life April 4, 1790, aged 76 years. Also his mother **Magdelen Tressey** who died May 22, 1806, aged 79 years.

3. [Flat]. Erected by **Patrick Treacy** in memory of his father **Anthony Treacy** who deceased March 4th, 1812 [?], aged 88 years. Also his wife **Catherine Treacy** who deceased August 17th 1815 [?], aged 76 [?] years.

4. [Buried flat]. IHS. Erected by **Felix Leonard** of Corgrea [*sic*; Corgary] in memory of his wife **Isabella McAffrey** who departed this life 1st August 1835, aged 39 years. Also his second **Bridget Duffy** who departed this life 28th January 1879, aged 80 years.

Sample of a transcription of Old Slavin Graveyard, Inishmacsaint Parish, County Fermanagh, 2011.

Three Old Inishmacsaint Parish Graveyards

	A	B	C	D	E	F	G	H
1	Last	First	Birth	Death	Age	Locator	Ref.	*Nee*
49	Heesey	Flaval ?					C8-2	
50	James	Denis		1767			OS4-4	
51	K.	P.		1729			OS4-6	
52	Keasey	Cormack	c.1664	1734	70		C8-3	
53	Kelly	Michael					OS1-2	
54	Keoine	Bridget	c.1708	1762	54		OS6-9	
55	Keown	Bernard	c.1864	1880	16	Cornahiltie	OS4-9	
56	Keown	Daniel				Cornahiltie	OS4-9	
57	Kerrigan	Andrew					OS5-3	
58	Kerrigan	Hugh				Philadelphia	OS5-3	
59	Kerrigan	James					OS5-3	
60	Kerrigan	John					OS5-3	
61	Kerrigan	Patrick	c.1789	1869	80	Acres	OS5-3	
62	*Kerrigan*	Sarah	c.1788	1872	84	Acres	OS5-3	
63	Kerrigan	Thomas					OS5-3	
64	Kerrigan	William					OS5-3	
65	Koen	Owen		1725			OS3-7	
66	Kown	Catherine	c.1802 ?	1852 ?	50		OS10-5	
67	Koyan	Constant	c.1661	1749	88		OS7-8	
68	*Koyan*	Giles	c.1668	1713	45		OS7-8	Nanngan
69	*Koyen*	Catlin	c.1736	1756	20		OS5-1	Brinan
70	Koyen	Constant	c.1691 ?	1737	46 ?		OS3-8	
71	Koyen	Constant		183??			OS10 G	
72	Koyen	Constant	c.1705	1734	29		OS10-6	
73	Koyen	Cormick	c.1658	1738	80		OS4-7	
74	Koyen	Hugh					OS5-1	
75	*Leonard*	Bridget	c.1799	1879	80	Corgary	OS2-4	Duffy
76	Leonard	Felix				Corgary	OS2-4	
77	*Leonard*	Isabella	c.1796	1835	39	Corgary	OS2-4	McAffrey
78							C9-1	

Sample of the index of the Three Old Inishmacsaint Parish Graveyards, County Fermanagh, 2011.

Try to get your results published in a local history or genealogy journal, on the Internet, or self-publish it in hard copy. Be sure to give a copy of your cemetery index to the church or the agency that manages the cemetery, in order to help other visitors who are looking for their ancestors.

CONCLUSION

If you have followed the instructions, doing a thorough search of records in the country to which your Irish ancestors and their siblings came — and have systematically used the various Irish archives and facilities outlined in the previous chapters — you should be able to solve some of the genealogical mysteries of your Irish ancestors, at least for one or more of your family lines. You will find something on them, possibly even locating their townland and visiting it. However, so much depends on the state of the records for the county you are researching. Even if you are a seasoned genealogist, you are not likely to get your whole Irish genealogy accomplished in one trip. This makes a good excuse for going back to Ireland.

One thing should stand out after you have read this book: there are vast untapped resources for genealogical research in Ireland, although they cannot replace the lost parish registers and the censuses. Other government documents, poor law union registers, and cemetery records, if used properly, can fill in many of the information gaps for your Irish ancestors.

I cannot over-emphasize that you need to get more than just BMDs (births, marriages, and deaths) for your research. You want to do family history, not only just genealogy. To understand the circumstances under which your ancestors lived in Ireland, you need to immerse yourself in the history and culture of Ireland. That is why I have included information on the museums and the historic sites that illustrate the history and physical culture of the Irish people.

As you are doing your research in any archives, whether in your home country or Ireland, it is important to record your sources. On the back of the photocopies, write the name of the archives, the name of the books, or the microfilm and document numbers. Having this information will save you time if you want to re-examine document collections.

As you process your data, enter it into a genealogy program such as Family Tree Maker, Legacy, or PAF (Personal Ancestry File). Scanned copies of the documents can be attached to the appropriate person's scrapbook in the genealogy program. This helps keep track of your materials.

I have emphasized working backward in time with documents from where our ancestors last lived. You need to establish a chain of evidence to make sure that you have the correct linkages once you begin working with the Irish documents.

With many primary Irish documents now on the Internet or LDS microfilms, you might be able to place your family in a county, a parish, and on a townland without even leaving your country, but there is so much more that you can learn by actually working in the Irish archives, handling the original documents, and seeing their context. By examining document collections, you can discover things that the Internet will miss because of spelling variations of surnames and townlands.

As you enter data into your computer, it is important to keep in mind issues surrounding genealogical "proof." It is so tempting to jump to conclusions by identifying someone as an ancestor because he or she had the right name, or lived on the same town-land. The person might be related, but could be a cousin, uncle, or great aunt, because several generations could live on the same townland, and if each son named his firstborn son after his father, you will find many cousins sharing the same names. You may have to do an extensive study of the parish register entries for all the people on that townland in order to sort out who is who. An example of such a study is the author's *A Comprehensive Index to the Devenish Church of Ireland Parish Registers, County Fermanagh.*

Your genealogical linkages need to be validated by actual documentation involving more than one primary source. Let me recommend Brenda Dougall Merriman's *Genealogical Standards of Evidence* as an important discussion of the problems of genealogi-cal verification. The Legacy family tree program allows you to rank your data by degrees of "proof."

In solving genealogical mysteries, you need to keep an open mind and avoid tunnel vision. You need to create hypotheses and test them against the evidence. If you find someone in the Irish records, is that really the person you are looking for? You need to try to verify or eliminate the person by following all the records that he or she generated in Ireland.

In Irish research, as in any genealogical research, you cannot presume things. Just because a person was living on a particular townland when he or she got married, you cannot assume that he or she was born on that townland or even in that county. If the person has only listed Ireland as the birthplace, that is all you should enter into the computer program until you find a primary document — such as a baptismal record or a civil registration — that gives a specific birthplace.

Be wary of genealogical trees posted on the web; so many times they are not documented and are inaccurate. Do not post your information on the web unless you are completely satisfied that it is accurate. If you do put your tree on the Internet, do not include information on living individuals, because of privacy concerns.

In your research in Ireland, you will no doubt generate new questions and find new relatives or family members who also may have emigrated from Ireland. You will have to start again, researching them in their adopted country. Use the checklist in Appendix A, as you did with your original research, to gain more information about their Irish background. Their information may unlock other genealogical doors for you. For those newfound ancestors who stayed in Ireland, you will have to go through the systematic process of finding everything you can about them in the Irish records, using the checklist in Appendix B.

Your Irish research may become a lifelong passion, as it has with me! I leave you with this Irish blessing:

> "Bless you and yours
> As well as the cottage you live in
> May the roof overhead be well-thatched
> And those inside be well-matched."

APPENDIX A

What to Research Before You Go to Ireland

- ☐ oral traditions
- ☐ family Bible
- ☐ family papers and correspondence
- ☐ family photos
- ☐ baptism and marriage certificates brought from Ireland
- ☐ marriage registrations in chosen country
- ☐ insurance applications
- ☐ death registrations
- ☐ death registrations of their children
- ☐ obituaries
- ☐ news items
- ☐ burial authorization
- ☐ church's burial register
- ☐ funeral home records
- ☐ funeral cards
- ☐ tombstones
- ☐ probated wills
- ☐ local histories
- ☐ historical atlases
- ☐ censuses

- ☐ lodge memberships
- ☐ church membership transfers
- ☐ passenger lists
- ☐ border crossings
- ☐ court records
- ☐ ships' departure manifests
- ☐ immigration records
- ☐ naturalization records
- ☐ passport applications
- ☐ bank records
- ☐ employment records
- ☐ land grant petitions
- ☐ homestead entries
- ☐ school records
- ☐ military attestations
- ☐ military medals
- ☐ Commonwealth War Graves Commission
- ☐ Legion obituaries, e.g. *Last Post*
- ☐ British or Scottish censuses
- ☐ British or Scottish civil registrations
- ☐ British military pension records
- ☐ British chaplains' returns of baptisms, marriages, and burials
- ☐ Royal Irish Constabulary service records
- ☐ home children records
- ☐ Irish Family History Foundation
- ☐ *www.findmypast.ie*
- ☐ *www.irishgenealogy.ie*
- ☐ Ulster Historical Foundation
- ☐ *www.irishtimes.com/ancestry*
- ☐ repeat research for siblings and cousins
- ☐ repeat research on neighbours if necessary

APPENDIX B

Things to Research While in Ireland

- [ ] Irish civil registrations of birth, marriages, and deaths
- [ ] parish registers
- [ ] marriage bonds
- [ ] marriage banns
- [ ] bishops' transcripts/returns
- [ ] confirmation lists
- [ ] vestry minutes
- [ ] cemeteries
- [ ] obituaries
- [ ] probated wills
- [ ] coroner's inquests
- [ ] memorials inside churches
- [ ] 1901 and 1911 censuses
- [ ] earlier census fragments
- [ ] religious censuses
- [ ] Tithe Applotments
- [ ] Ordnance Survey field books
- [ ] OS Maps with numbers that link with *Griffith's Valuation*
- [ ] *Griffith's Valuation*
- [ ] revision or cancellation books

- ☐ Environmental Protection Agency maps
- ☐ land leases
- ☐ land deeds
- ☐ other memorials at Registry of Deeds
- ☐ estate papers
- ☐ assisted emigration lists
- ☐ arrival lists for British ports
- ☐ personal papers in archives
- ☐ freeholder's lists
- ☐ hearth tax rolls
- ☐ employment records
- ☐ law firm records
- ☐ Landed Estates Court Rental investigations
- ☐ news items
- ☐ school records
- ☐ Trinity College Dublin alumni lists
- ☐ Rebellion losses
- ☐ Rebellion trials
- ☐ militia lists
- ☐ IRA membership lists
- ☐ First World War military memorial books for Ireland
- ☐ Royal Irish Constabulary service records
- ☐ various permits — for possessing guns, for example
- ☐ town and city directories
- ☐ tradesmen guilds
- ☐ professional associations
- ☐ lodge memberships
- ☐ coats of arms
- ☐ local histories
- ☐ poor law union workhouse records
- ☐ poor law union outdoor relief registers
- ☐ poor law union health registers

☐ board of guardians minutes
☐ clergy directories
☐ political party records
☐ British Parliamentary Sessional Papers
☐ British civil registrations
☐ British censuses
☐ Scottish old parish registers and civil registrations
☐ Scottish censuses
☐ old age pension searches of 1841–1851 censuses
☐ old age pension searches of parish registers
☐ research ancestors' siblings and cousins

APPENDIX C

Important Historical and Genealogical Websites for Irish Research

$$$, £££, €€€ = subscription or pay-per-view in dollars, pounds, or euros.

www.ancestry.com: $$$. This premier site has census and civil registrations for England, Canada, and the United States, as well as passenger lists and military records. Many of its digital images can be downloaded. Its Irish section is developing. You can access this site at libraries for free.

www.ancestryireland.com: £££. The Ulster Historical Foundation operates a research service in Belfast, has a large database of materials pertinent to Northern Ireland, and publishes important books on Irish history and genealogy. Membership in this foundation allows you to search its linked site, History from Headstones. The organization also operates a summer school to introduce you to the important archives and repositories in Ulster.

www.askaboutireland.ie: This site has images of the *Griffith's Valuation* for all of Ireland and associated maps for the townlands in the Republic.

www.bdm.nsw.gov.au/familyHistory: A listing of vital records for New South Wales.

www.belfastcity.gov.uk/burialrecords: Indexes of burials that took place in Belfast with information on last known address.

www.campingireland.ie: If you decide to camp in Ireland, this site will show you what is available in most counties.

www.collectionscanada.gc.ca: Library and Archives Canada has many free databases for census, immigration, land petition indexes, and military attestation papers. Many of the documents have been digitized and are downloadable.

www.corkarchives.ie/genealogy: The genealogy section of the Cork City and County Archives.

www.cwgc.org: Commonwealth War Graves Commission. Its database holds information on the deaths of Irish soldiers in the First and Second World Wars and next of kin.

www.derry.rootsireland.ie: £££. Established by the genealogy centre in Londonderry, this site has a large pay-per-view database for County Londonderry.

www.dippam.ac.uk: This site has British parliamentary papers pertaining to Ireland and Irish migration records.

www.dunbrody.com: The Dunbody Famine Ship exhibit, County Wexford.

www.dunfanghy.com: Situated in the extreme northwest of County Donegal, this Famine museum is set in the old workhouse.

www.ellisisland.org: A database of people entering the United States through New York City.

www.emeraldancestors.com: £££. A database dealing primarily with Ulster.

www.eneclann.ie: Eneclann is a professional genealogical research firm in Dublin that also publishes databases on CD-ROM.

www.familysearch.org: The genealogical site of the Church of Jesus Christ of Latter-Day Saints (Mormons). It has many of the Irish civil registrations of births, marriages, and deaths indexed online up to the end of 1921 for the whole country, and from 1922 onward for the Republic.

www.findmypast.co.uk: £££. It has indexes of English censuses, civil registrations, military pension records, military BMDs from throughout the British empire, outbound passenger lists, etc. It can be very useful for Irish research.

www.findmypast.ie: €€€. This new site, in conjunction with Eneclann, has digitized land and estate records, the *Griffith's Valuation*, directories, military and rebellion documents, migration records, wills, and more to come.

www.globalgenealogy.com: A publisher and seller of genealogical books, CDs, and materials.

www.gro.gov.uk/gro.content/certificates: £££. General Registry Office for Britain. Here you can get British vital certificates as well as military births, marriages, and baptisms recorded in Ireland and elsewhere.

www.groireland.ie: €€€. The official site of the General Registry Office of Ireland in the town of Roscommon, County Roscommon. You can download its forms for civil registrations and fax your requests to this office if you know the reference numbers for the vital registrations. It covers all of Ireland up to the end of 1921 and for the Republic from 1922. It is cheaper than using GRONI in Belfast.

www.groni.gov.uk: £££. The General Registry Office of Northern Ireland in Belfast. It carries only vital records for Northern Ireland. Certificates can be ordered online. If you do not know the dates of the events, a two-year search will be done.

www.heritageireland.ie/en: The Office of the Public Works manages many of the heritage sites throughout the Republic. Its Heritage Card can be used to enter more than one hundred sites.

www.ingeneas.com: $$$. A Canadian site dealing with immigration.

www.inhp.com: Irish National Heritage Park, County Wexford.

www.ireland genealogy.com: £££. This site has extracts of the searches of the 1841 and 1851 censuses for Old Age Pension applications.

www.ireland.anglican.org: The official site for the Church of Ireland. It has links to its clergy, churches, and archives.

www.irishgenealogy.ie: Has over two million Church of Ireland parish records for Counties Cork, Kerry, Carlow, and the city of Dublin.

www.irishmethodist.org: The Methodist Historical Society in Belfast.

www.irishorigins.com: £££. Part of the Origins Network, this site has *Griffith's Valuation* and other important Irish documents that you can download.

www.irishtimes.com/ancestor: €€€. Using the *Griffith's Valuation* and other documents, this site allows you to search for occurrences of several different surnames in the same place, allowing you to identify where your ancestors might have come from.

www.kinfolkfinders.com: The website of the author's research company, listing parish registers and cemetery indexes published.

www.movinghere.og.uk: A site containing many Irish records held in the British archives.

www.nationalarchives.ie: The National Archives of Ireland in Dublin. Online 1901 and 1911 censuses, as well as other important sources of information.

www.nifhs.org: £££. The North of Ireland Family History Society Research Centre in Belfast. Use of its research room is limited to its members.

www.nli.ie: The National Library of Ireland in Dublin. Its catalogue and many other resources are listed on this site.

www.nmni.com.uftm: The Ulster Folk and Transportation Museum, Culta, County Down.

www.nmni.com.uafp: The Ulster Amercan Folk Park, Omagh, County Tyrone.

www.nmni.com/um: The award-winning Ulster Museum in Belfast.

www.ogs.on.ca: The Ontario Genealogical Society's website. See its special interest groups for Irish and Irish Palatine research.

http://paperofrecord.hypernet.ca: Paper of Record has digitized many international newspapers, including the *Irish Canadian*.

www.presbyterianhistoryireland.com: Presbyterian Historical Society in Belfast.

www.progenealogists.com: This site lists the surviving Church of Ireland parish registers.

www.proni.gov.uk: The Public Records Office of Northern Ireland in Belfast. On it are many databases and indexes, digitized images of Freeholders' lists, Ulster Covenant, and wills that you can download. Its online catalogue is very helpful.

www.psni.police.uk/index/about-us/police_museum/museum_genealogy: £££. This site allows you to order extracts of the Royal Irish Constabulary service records.

www.quakers-in-ireland.ie: You can contact the Quaker Archives in Dublin through this site.

www.quab.ac.uk/cms: Centre for Migration Studies, County Tyrone.

www.qub.ac.uk: Queen's University, Belfast.

www.rootsireland.ie: €€€. The Irish Family History Foundation has extracted many of the parish registers, civil registrations, and census records. This pay-per-view site can be very expensive to use and the results disappointing, because it has only a fraction of the sources available. The search engines are being improved, but you can only download an extract of the document, not the original image.

www.scotlandspeople.gov.uk: £££. This has Scottish censuses, early parish registers, wills, and civil registrations. Because of the movement back and forth between Ireland and Scotland, this site may be important to your Irish research.

www.seanruad.com: The IreAtlas Townland database is very useful for locating townlands in counties, parishes, baronies, and poor law unions.

www.stevemorse.com: A powerful search engine for Castle Garden and Ellis Island immigration data.

www.strokestownpark.ie/museum: A premier Famine museum in County Roscommon.

www.summeratucd.ie: The booking site for the dormitories of University College Dublin.

www.tcd.ie/Library: Trinity College Dublin's library site will give you information on its holdings.

www.ulsterancestry.com: A professional genealogy service that also has a large, free database for Northern Ireland.

www.valoff.ie: The Valuation Office in Dublin.

www.wicklowhistoricalgoal.com: Visiting this old prison, in the town of Wicklow, Wicklow County, is a very moving experience.

ANNOTATED BIBLIOGRAPHY

A Handlist of Church of Ireland Parish Registers in the Representative Church Body Library Dublin. Dublin: RCB Library, 2011. A list of parish registers and copies arranged by county.

Bannon, Edel, Louise McLaughlin and Cecilia Flanagan, eds. *Boho Heritage: A Treasure Trove of History and Lore.* Enniskillen: Boho Heritage Organization, 2009. This local history of Boho Parish, County Fermanagh, sets the standard for local histories. Each of the townlands in the parish has its own chapter. Each chapter has family histories, photographs, maps, population charts, and the *Griffith's Valuation.*

Cahill, Thomas. *How the Irish Saved Civilization.* New York: Anchor Books, 1995. A good coverage of medieval Ireland.

Day, Angélique and Patrick McWiliams, eds. *Ordnance Survey Memoirs of Ireland.* 40 vols. Belfast: The Institute of Irish Studies, Queen's University, Belfast, 1990. The research for this series, done in the 1830s, gives an important glimpse into the geography, history, and culture of Northern Ireland and parts of Donegal, often mentioning the names of people and their townlands. There is an extensive index in a separate volume. There is unpublished information on some of the counties of the Republic available at the Royal Irish Institute in Dublin.

Discoverer Maps. Belfast: Ordnance Survey of Northern Ireland. A series of twenty-nine maps that show the roads and many of the townlands in current Ulster. These are important as you explore the back roads. Folded into a 4½-by-7-inch size, they can be put into your pocket for handy reference and *Griffith's Valuation* details.

Discovery Maps. Dublin: Ordnance Survey of Ireland. A similar series of sixty maps covering the Republic of Ireland. As of the summer of 2011, the *Discovery Maps* had not incorporated the recent additional M-series highways.

Elliott, Bruce S. *Irish Migrants in the Canada: A New Approach.* Kingston and Montreal: McGill-Queen's University Press, 1988. The author explores block and chain migration of 775 families from Counties Tipperary and Offaly.

Elliott, David R. *A Comprehensive Index to the Devenish Church of Ireland Parish Registers, County Fermanagh.* Parkhill, Ontario: Kinfolk Finders, 2011. There are two indexes of the parish registers in this book; the first lists all of the people alphabetically by surname and forename; the second lists people by surname according to their townland and chronologically. This way, the family units on each townland can be seen. Over six thousand baptisms, marriages, and burials indexed. Available in hardcover and CD-ROM.

_____. *Enniskillen Poor Law Union Outdoor Relief Register (1848– 1899).* Parkhill, Ontario: Kinfolk Finders, 2009. This contains almost three thousand names of people from parts of Counties Fermanagh, Tyrone, and Cavan who received relief outside of the workhouse during the Great Famine and beyond.

_____. *The Cemetery of St. Molaise, Monea, Devenish Parish, County Fermanagh.* Parkhill, Ontario: Kinfolk Finders, 2006. This was the first of about twenty cemetery indexes published by Kinfolk Finders. Some of the examples from it have been used in chapter seven.

_____. *Three Old Inishmacsaint Parish Graveyards: Inishmacsaint Island, Carrick, and Old Slavin*. Parkhill, Ontario: Kinfolk Finders, 2011. Some of its photos, tombstone transcriptions, and index were used in chapter seven.

General Alphabetical Index to the Townlands and Towns, Parishes, and Baronies of Ireland. Dublin: Alexander Thom, 1861; reprinted by Genealogical Publishing Co., Inc., Baltimore, 2000. This is the Bible for Irish genealogical research, linking the over sixty thousand Irish townlands to their parishes, counties, baronies, poor law unions, and the Ordnance Survey maps and giving their area size.

Grenham, John. *Tracing Your Irish Ancestors: The Complete Guide*. 3rd edition. Dublin: Gill and Macmillan, 2006. This work is essential for Irish genealogical work. Grenham provides information on many of the resources found in the Irish archives and libraries. His list of Roman Catholic parish register microfilms and their dates is extremely important if you are tracking Catholic ancestors. The author has a fourth edition in the works.

Handran, George B. *Townlands in Poor Law Unions*. Salem: Higginson Book Company, 1997. Good for placing townlands in their electoral districts.

Herlihy, Jim. *The Royal Irish Constabulary*. Dublin: Four Courts Press, 1997. By a serving member of the Garda, this book lists the names and service numbers of over 83,000 officers of the RIC. It also informs you on how to obtain their service records. He has also published a similar work on the Dublin Metropolitan Police.

Holt, Ruth and Margaret Williams. *Genealogical Extractions and*

Index of the Canada Company Remittance Books, 1843–1847. Weston, Ontario: R. Holt, 1990. This is an index of the names and addresses of senders and recipients for money transfers conducted by the Canada Company for people who wanted to send money back to their relatives and friends in the British Isles. The Canada Company had offices in the larger cities of Ireland. The original remittance records, stored in the Archives of Ontario, can be found under the following archival reference code F 129, C-7, Vols. 1–7.

Hood, Susan. *Royal Roots Republican Inheritance: The Survival of the Office of Arms.* Dublin: Woodfield Press, 2002. The author traces the transition of Britain's Heraldry Office at Dublin Castle to the Genealogy Office under the direction of the National Library following Home Rule in 1922.

Hoppen, K. Theodore. *Ireland Since 1800: Conflicts and Conformity.* New York: Longman Publishing, 1989. This book explores the historiography of Ireland, its myths and realities. It is strong on the religio-political social history, shedding new light on the Famine period and beyond by using new models of statistical analysis.

Leslie, J.B. *Clergy of Clogher: Biographical Succession Lists.* Revised edition. Belfast: Ulster Historical Foundation, 2006. This work on the Church of Ireland in the Diocese of Clogher provides biographical data on its clergy and the history of the churches in that diocese. The Ulster Historical Foundation, in conjunction with the Representative Church Body, has published similar volumes on the clergy in some of the other dioceses of Ireland; however, they lack the historical infor-mation on the churches themselves.

Lewis, Samuel. *A Topographical Dictionary of Ireland.* London: Samuel Lewis and Co., 1842. It provides historical and geographic information on many of the towns and cities in Ireland for the 1830s when the research was done. This will give you background on what your ancestors would have experienced during that time. You can find this valuable book on the Internet and also on CD-ROM (by Global Genealogy).

MacKay, Donald. *Flight from Famine: The Coming of the Irish to Canada*. Toronto: Natural Heritage Books, 2009. The author examines the social background to: assisted emigration from Ireland in the 1830s through to the Great Famine, and the experiences of those settlers in Ontario.

Maxwell, Ian. *Tracing your Ancestors in Northern Ireland: A Guide to Ancestry Research in the Public Records Office of Northern Ireland*. Edinburgh: The Stationary Office, 1997. Now made out of date by PRONI's move and computerization, this work still gives a good coverage of PRONI's official and private holdings.

Memorial Atlas of Ireland, 1901. Philadelphia. L.J. Richards, 1901. The atlas depicts the Irish provinces, parishes, baronies, towns, cities, and landmarks as they were in 1901. In 2011, Global Genealogy published it on CD-ROM.

Merriman, Brenda Dougall. *Genealogical Standards of Evidence: A Guide for Family Historians*. Toronto: Ontario Genealogical Society and Dundurn Press, 2010. The author stresses the importance of evidence when constructing genealogical linkages between people. She explains the differences between original and derivative sources, primary and secondary information, direct and indirect evidence, the preponderance of evidence, and the Genealogical Proof Standard.

Mitchell, Brian. *A New Genealogical Atlas of Ireland*. Second edition. Baltimore: Genealogical Publishing Co. Inc., 2003. An excellent series of maps of the counties, baronies, dioceses, parishes, Roman Catholic parishes, townlands, and probate districts, with definitions of these divisions.

_____. *Finding your Irish Ancestors: Unique Aspects of Irish Genealogy*.

Baltimore: Clearfield Company, 2001. A series of eight published lectures by this specialist in Irish genealogy in which
he talks about the peculiar problems you can encounter in
doing Irish genealogy and how to overcome them. Somewhat
dated, it looked forward to the large computer databases covering all of Ireland.

_____. *Pocket Guide to Irish Genealogy*. Third edition. Baltimore:
Clearfield Company, 2008. The author presents a number of
case studies and explains the types of Irish and non-Irish
records he used to undertake the genealogical research. The
costs of using GRONI in Belfast need to be updated.

O'Connor, Michael H. *A Guide to Tracing Your Kerry Ancestors*.
Dublin: Flyleaf Books, 1990. This book provides information on doing genealogical work in County Kerry, listing
the official and local resources including cemetery transcripts.
The publisher has produced similar books for other counties
written by different authors.

Official Road Atlas Ireland. Dublin and Belfast: Ordnance Survey
of Ireland and the Ordnance Survey of Northern Ireland,
2011. An important source for travel in Ireland with the new
M-series highways included and the renumbering of some of
the former N-series highways. It also has maps of the larger
towns and cities.

Philip's Street Atlas: Co Tyrone and Co Fermanagh. London: Philips
Maps, 2006. An excellent atlas of the location of townlands
in these counties. This company has published two similar
atlases covering counties Londonderry and Antrim, and
Down and Armagh.

Póirtéir, Cathal, ed. *The Great Irish Famine*. Dublin: RTE and Mercier
Press, 1995. A symposium, part of the Thomas Davis Lecture
Series, gives a wide-ranging social history of the famine.

Radford, Dwight A. and Kyle J. Betit. *Discovering your Irish*

Ancestors. Cincinnati: Betterway Books, 2001. This publication illustrates the types of documents available in the countries of Irish emigrants that will help you identify their county of origin in Ireland. It is especially good on Canadian and American sources of information.

Raymond, Stuart A. *Irish Family History on the Web: A Directory.* Second edition. Bury, England: The Federation of Family History Societies, 2006. This book lists websites for the Irish genealogical societies by county, parish registers, cemetery indexes, and other online resources, including those in Britain, Canada, and the United States. Although some of the websites may have changed, this book will provide you with a view of how much of a role the Internet now plays in Irish genealogy.

Refausse, Raymond. *Church of Ireland Records.* Second edition. Dublin: Four Courts Press, 2006. By the archivist of the RCB (Representative Church Body) Library in Dublin, this gives a good background on the Church of Ireland and the type of documents it generated.

Ryan, James. *Irish Records: Sources for Family and Local History.* Revised Edition Salt Lake City: *Ancestry.com,* 1997. Somewhat dated, this book lists the denominational parish registers for each county, as well as books, unpublished manuscripts, and journal articles pertaining to those counties available in the National Library, National Archives, and PRONI.

Wells, Ronald A. *Friendship Towards Peace: The Journey of Ken Newell and Gerry Reynolds.* Dublin: The Columba Press, 2005. This is the remarkable story of the two Belfast clergy who worked for peace in their troubled country.

Woodham-Smith, Cecil. *The Great Hunger: Ireland 1845–1849.* New York: Harper & Row, Publishers, 1962. This scholarly and highly readable study of the Great Famine depicts the political, economic, and social context of the period.

INDEX

All page entries in italics indicate that the
subject is in an image or on a map.

OF RELATED INTEREST

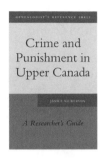

Crime and Punishment in Upper Canada
A Researcher's Guide
Janice Nickerson
978-1554887705

Crime and Punishment in Upper Canada provides genealogists and social historians with context and tools to understand the criminal justice system and locate sources on criminal activity and its consequences for the Upper Canada period (1791–1841) of Ontario's history.

Illustrative examples further aid researchers in this era of the province's past, which is notoriously difficult to investigate due to paucity of records and indexes. An entertaining, educational read, the book features chapters with detailed inventories of available records in federal, provincial, and local repositories; published transcripts and indexes; online transcripts and indices; and suggestions for additional reading.

Also included are engravings (jails and courthouses, public hangings, judges), maps (showing the boundaries of districts), charts (for statistics such as frequencies of different kinds of offences), and document examples (court minutes, jail registers, newspaper reports, et cetera), while case studies demonstrate the use and relevance of various records.

A Call to
the Colours

A Call to the Colours
Tracing Your Canadian Military Ancestors
Kenneth G. Cox
978-1554888641

Beginning in Canada's earliest days, our ancestors were required to perform some form of military service, often as militia. The discovery that an ancestor served during one of the major conflicts in our history is exciting. When you find a family name on a Loyalist muster roll, a Canada General Service Medal with an ancestor's name engraved on it, a set of First World War attestation papers, or a box of Second World War medals, you realize that one of your ancestors faced challenging events beyond the scope of ordinary living. There are ways to trace their journeys and thus flesh out a more complete story of the history of your family.

A Call to the Colours provides the archival, library, and computer resources that can be employed to explore your family's military history, using items such as old photographs, documents, uniforms, medals, and other militaria to guide the search. The book is generously illustrated with examples of the sorts of artifacts and documents you can find.

Conserving, Preserving, and Restoring Your Heritage
A Professional's Advice
Kennis Kim
978-1554884629

Artifacts, whether found in museums, our community, or our homes, offer glimpses into the past. Be they documents, photographs, books, or clothing, as custodians of our history, we're faced with how to maintain these items. Professional conservator Kennis Kim tells us how. Topics discussed include: creating an accession list; the nature of conservation, restoration, and preservation; deciding on display, storage, or using the artifact; common threats such as light, humidity, insects, and rodents; and when to call a professional. Here is all that's needed to determine what can be done to preserve precious articles for future generations.

ALSO BY DAVID R. ELLIOTT

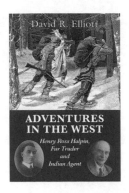

Adventures in the West
Henry Halpin, Fur Trader and Indian Agent
978-1550028034

This is the story of Irish-born Henry Ross Halpin, who by the age of 16 began a long association with the fur trade and Canada's native peoples, was thrice employed by the Hudson's Bay Company, and became an Indian agent (1885–1901). Halpin's work took him from Fort Garry, Manitoba, to Fort York on the shores of the Hudson Bay, and across the Prairies to British Columbia.

Available at your favourite bookseller.

DUNDURN
www.dundurn.com

What did you think of this book? Visit www.dundurn.com
for reviews, videos, updates, and more!

Marquis Book Printing Inc.

Québec, Canada
2012